A DISC & MOTIVATORS GUIDE TO

UNDERSTANDING *Me* UNDERSTANDING *You*

KEYS TO TRANSFORMING RELATIONSHIPS

WENDY CRAWFORD

DEDICATION

This book is dedicated to God, the One who truly transforms lives and has transformed mine. He is the One who sent His messengers to encourage me to write this book and gave me the grace to complete it so quickly. I also dedicate this book to my amazing husband, Dan, and my three wonderful children, Riley, Ellie, and Josiah. Each one of you in your own unique way have taught me so much about love and life. Sharing life with you has enriched me profoundly and helped me to grow personally in so many ways. To each one of you I am forever grateful. I love you all so much!

ACKNOWLEDGMENTS

DAN CRAWFORD: As an amazing husband, father, friend, you have sacrificed so much through the years to provide for our family. Because of this, each one of us is able to be and do more for God. You have made a way for me to "be there" for the kids. Thank you for your love, support, and making dreams come true! I love you so!

DANNY SILK: Your passion, wisdom, and knowledge are gifts which truly transform lives. As a family, we have been impacted profoundly by your messages. We are forever changed! Thank you for personally encouraging and inviting me to partner with you at *Loving on Purpose*. What a honor and blessing for which I'm so grateful!

LAURIE VANGELDER: I love who you are! I am so grateful for your friendship and for your amazing gift to see, hear, and connect people whom God wants connected. You are His voice and have His eyes to see what He wants to orchestrate. I would not be where I am today without you! I cannot thank you enough! Love you, friend!

JASON HEDGE: I'm thankful for your heart to develop people, your hospitality, and for always promoting me as well. Also, for listening to my heart and allowing me to connect and be a part of what God is doing through Bethel to bring heaven to earth. Thank you for your friendship and honor for which I'm so thankful!

JACKIE DURANT: I love your passion and simply who you are. It's been such a joy to get to know you and to see all the arms of HOPE City grow and develop because of your faithfulness. I'm so thankful for the opportunities and places you've given me to "happen." Thank you so much! I treasure you!

DAVE AND LUANNE SMITH: You both bless me beyond measure! I've longed for covenant relationships and you've shown me what that looks like. Thank you for your support and for coaching me through some of my rawest moments. I thank God for you both!

ANDY MASON AND TONY STOLTZFUS: Thank you for encouraging me to write a book on this topic and for your experience in going before me and showing me the way.

ALL OF YOU FROM MY HOSANNA! DAYS: You know who you are and the list is long! So many of you have touched me and contributed to my life in many ways—from the early days when I first came to know the Lord through the various seasons of growth, ministry, training, and equipping. Thank you for your friendship, encouragement, and for equipping me to teach, coach, and minister to others as well. I thank each one of you for sowing into my life!

KAY COULTER: Thank you so much for your expertise as my editor, for your great communications, hard work, and timeliness. Thank you for working long, hard hours to turn this book around in such a short period of time. You've been a joy to work with! You were an answer to prayer! I'm so glad God led me to you!

CINDY KACHER: My precious friend, you are an incredible blessing and gift to me. I have learned so much simply by spending time with you. Thank you for being there to pour through this book–one more time–with a fresh set of eyes. There's not enough words to properly express the richness of our friendship and what you mean to me.

SOMMER SLONEKER: I'm so thankful God brought you into my life! You bless me beyond measure and are a dear friend. Thank you for your eagle eyes on this as well. I'm so grateful for you. It's been such a joy getting to know you as we journey together through life.

ENDORSEMENTS

I really appreciate the style and readability of Wendy's writing. From the beginning she engages you in what will be a transformational journey. I have seen her at work. Wendy did a full assessment of the Leadership Team in my church followed by a seminar and the results were astounding. Through her skills and teaching we discovered so much about our team and how to make better connections, to function in our gifting, to understand the how and why of the things we do (or don't do!) and she raised the level of our awareness in understanding and appreciating different styles of functioning in all our relationships.

In the first two chapters Wendy sets the stage for clearly understanding the technical aspects of the DISC and Motivators Assessment, what they show you and how they can help you. Like she says "communication with each other is much like speaking in foreign languages" and in this book she has given us the principles of interpretation.

If you hunger for that, then this book will challenge you and enable you to take it the next level in your family, team, or life. I would wholeheartedly encourage you to, first read this book, and also to have Wendy come to your church. Take the assessments and experience the transformation it will bring to you and your church. We are thankful for all the help and revelation Wendy brought to us. We are not the same, we have been changed and it is GOOD!

MICHAEL MEHRING
Senior Pastor
Full Gospel Church
Walworth, WI

Wendy Crawford not only has an in-depth understanding of DISC Behaviors and Motivators but also has an articulate ability to present this information in a way that is both informative and enjoyable. I have been a recipient of her training and also observed her apply this material in coaching a number of my colleagues. I am greatly impressed at the results of her instruction and coaching. Colleagues have been able to better find their fit and also communicate what they need in order to operate as part of our high-functioning teams. I would have no hesitation recommending this book or any of Wendy's resources if you are wanting to gain a better understanding of personal behavioral styles and learn skills to improve your ability to communicate with others.

ANDY MASON
Global Transformation Institute
Bethel Church, Redding, CA
Author of *Dream Culture: Bringing Dreams to Life*
idreamculture.com

This book will certainly send you on a mission of discovering your identity as it relates to how God uniquely designed you even down to the most integral detail. Once this happens you can begin to see a paradigm shift in your circumstances, your surroundings, particularly your purpose, your families, and relationships, but most importantly your calling to bring God glory. Scripture teaches us that "the truth will set you free." My friends, this book will speak clearly and directly into the rich life the Lord is calling you to live. Now is the time to find it!

SUSAN FANNON
Connecting Pastor
Hosanna! Church
Lakeville, MN

Wendy's guidance and wisdom has had a significant impact on how we communicate and relate to each other as a married couple. She helped us to understand and appreciate how we are uniquely created as individuals. She gave us a new set of communication tools that has taken our marriage to another level. Once we saw how powerful the impact was on our marriage, we had her come and work with the entire team at our organization, which was a huge success. Our team learned to interact with one another at a greater level and gained a new appreciation for each person's unique gifting, which ultimately resulted in a happier work environment!

JOEL AND JANIE TAYLOR
Managing Director
Bethel Music / WorshipU
bethelmusic.com
Redding, CA

Wendy's talent is a gift from God, given to her to help others. The info given in her workshops is communicated in a way that is so captivating and useful that I could not be more excited to hear she has taken the time to put it in book form so it can be shared with the masses. This book will be a valuable tool for anyone on the planet who desires practical insight and understanding of relationship behavioral styles and motivation.

The workshop Wendy conducted for us was an important part of our recent hiring process but the info we gleaned about each member of our team went well beyond that in strengthening our communication with one another and being able to celebrate our differences. It has really brought our team together.

LAURIE VANGELDER
New Day Church
New Prague, MN

Having worked with Wendy in a variety of church training settings and in other professional trainings, I have been impressed each time with not only her professionalism and grasp of the content she brings, but especially by her ability to listen well, adapt the excellent materials to the audience, and bring practical challenges that result in real and positive life-change. Follow up surveys we have done with participants in her trainings have consistently demonstrated the value of what Wendy brings. Personally, the knowledge I have gained from DISC has changed how I teach and how I counsel. Wendy's presentation of the DISC is clear, practical, and will benefit the relationships of all who read it.

PASTOR JIM BUSSCHER
Adult Life Events Pastor
Hosanna! Church
Lakeville, MN

Wendy facilitated discussions with our Management Team on understanding each of our individual DISC Behaviors and Motivators Assessments. Once the team came to a wonderful respectful understanding of each other, Wendy moved us to the next level of how to use this information when communicating within the team. These discussions have helped us become a more cohesive team and also gave us new and important insights into ourselves which have been so helpful. Overall great outcomes for moving our team and TreeHouse forward.

REBECCA L. WALKER
Executive Director
TreeHouse
treehouseyouth.org
Edina, MN

I am excited to see that Wendy has made DISC practical and accessible for families through *Understanding Me, Understanding You*. My wife and I identified the behavior styles of our kids early on, and it was a huge benefit in adapting the way we parented to their unique personalities. With an I/D (she has a plan for your life) and an S/C (who goes along to get along), they were very, very different, and what worked for one would often be a disaster for the other. Now that they are adults, knowing each other's DISC brings a wealth of understanding and insight to our family interactions. If you are a parent, you need this book. I don't know of any other tool that can bring as much benefit to understanding each other in your family than learning your DISC behavior styles.

TONY STOLTZFUS
Founder and Director of Leadership MetaFormation and Coach22
Author of eight books, including: *Coaching Questions*
Leadership Coaching
The Calling Journey

I had known Wendy Crawford for more than four years, when we enlisted her as a consultant. Our team found her training to be very insightful and resourceful in helping us to make decisions as a church in terms of staff and direction. Wendy helped us to develop better systems of communication and all of our relationships are better because of her instruction. This book is one of those resources that you will keep going back to and each time you do, you will come away with a deeper understanding of yourself and those you are working with. I am sure all who read it will keep it close by as a resource for a long time.

DOYAL VANGELDER
Senior Pastor
New Day Church
New Prague, MN

Wendy has a mastery over this material like no one else I know. She has combined her passion for helping families reconnect and her knowledge of DISC to create a invaluable resource.

Each year Wendy spends hundreds hours meeting individually with couples and families to help them discover who they are how their differences bring value to one another. She has now brought that wisdom into book form enabling everyone else to benefit from the tools she has gathered over the years. As you read through this book, you will hear her heart for families and the lessons she has learned throughout her ministry time. You will also find the Lord's anointing woven into the pages revealing truths about how He created us with differences that complement each other when we intentionally use our gifts to bless and honor the ones we love.

I know you are going to value this resource as a foundational tool to improve and to take your relationships to the next level.

JASON HEDGE
Director of Human Resources
Senior Professional in Human Resources
Bethel Church
Redding, CA

Author of:
The Essential DISC Training Workbook
Founder of DISC-U.org

Wendy Crawford's Leadership Coaching Course came highly recommended, so I enrolled to learn how to more effectively lead my women's ministry team. I came away with much, much more. Wendy presented practical strategies to coaching with authenticity that immediately impacted my effectiveness as a leader. Her courses and workshops provided the retainable instruction I needed to create meaningful dialogue and achieve greater synergy in my work and personal relationships through all that I learned from DISC and Motivators. Training with Wendy got my team thinking outside our programmed responses to a more intuitive way of listening and understanding one another. It's been revolutionary! I highly recommend Wendy for life coaching, teambuilding and relational leadership training!

KIM SERBUS
Pastor Women's Ministry
Celebration Church
Lakeville, MN

*"If you talk to a man in a language he understands,
that goes to his head.
If you talk to him in his language,
that goes to his heart."*

~ Nelson Mandela ~

TABLE OF CONTENTS

FOREWORD

Any time we get more than one person in a room we soon discover that we are different. Sometimes the differences are intriguing and pleasant. But too often these differences cause us to wonder. We wonder what is wrong with this person that he or she would act this way. Somehow we fail to recognize the value and vitality that God has purposefully placed in the design of his creation. Anxiety is our experience in the face of these very natural diversities and complexities. These experiences aren't necessarily an encounter with a stranger. They are common occurrences in our own families. One of my favorite tools to help bring understanding and that helps to reduce this destructive anxiety is DISC. I have used this tool for many years helping diverse groups find strength and productivity in working together toward common goals.

What I love about this book is that Wendy is turning this tool into a "Total Family Makeover" experience! This is a direct result of her heart and passion to see families, marriages, and teams transformed. She has done something I've never seen done before. In all my work with marriages and families, I've never heard of someone effectively using DISC assessments with family, coaching, and action plans. In her book, *Understanding Me, Understanding You*, Wendy Crawford is going to take you deeper into a fabulous tool and then teach you how to connect with your own family and others at a higher level. A more effective style of communication, the ease with which family members live together and the revelation of what each person needs to thrive and excel will come to light as you turn these pages.

Generally, we approve of those things that we find in each other that remind us of the strengths we ourselves carry. We like to encourage the world around us to grow in the strengths that we understand and value in how to be successful in life. For example, if we are a slow decision maker, cautious about risk and careful to take in loads of information before committing ourselves to a decision, then we are supportive and understanding of our children who behave in a similar pattern. But, if one of our family members is more of the "Ready-FIRE-Aim" style of behavior and decision making, our anxieties climb through the roof when we cross paths with them. Oh, and we live in the same house as them so we cross paths all day long! This anxiety creates misunderstandings and those misunderstandings lead to disconnections. Our family life experience can be diluted by the simple reality that we are different now and always will be.

Traits, personalities and temperaments are avenues to results rather than results themselves. But, too often we see the behaviors in others that are different than the behaviors we choose and we judge people and our family members, according to the avenue instead of the result. Sometimes, we assign moral judgments to the behaviors that are different than ours simply because we don't understand why someone would choose another path. These exchanges can be brutal to our connections and create so much unnecessary anxiety.

Wendy brings clarity to the needs of family members who are so distinctly different. The way she presents this information helps the readers into the awareness of what is happening on the inside of the people they care so deeply about. She leads them into a new understanding of why each one responds so differently to the same situation. With this new found revelation, the family dynamics will change from angry, powerless and often hurtful reactions to thoughtful responses based on keen insight and careful decisions. Wendy's *Understanding Me, Understanding You* methods and training are key to improving your connections, relationships, and communication which will build a greater ease to relating to one another. Get ready to see your children, your spouse and the world around you differently as you allow Wendy to reintroduce yourself to yourself and in turn reintroduce you to your family and friends. Enjoy!

DANNY SILK
Founder of Loving on Purpose
Director of Bethel Staff Development
Global Transformation Institute
Bethel Church, Redding, CA

Author of:
Loving our Kids on Purpose
Culture of Honor
Defining the Relationship
Powerful & Free

INTRODUCTION

I am excited to share with you my heart and all I have learned over the years that has personally transformed my relationships and family. This all started somewhere in the eleventh year of my marriage. Both my husband and I were in the midst of our Coach Training Certification. In addition to Coach Training, I was learning all about TTI's (Target Training International) DISC Behaviors and Motivators assessment tools in preparation for certification.

After looking through my husband's assessment results, I had an epiphany moment. As plain as day on paper, I could see exactly where we were polar opposites. My assessment revealed that I am 95 percent on the C-scale, which means I am a highly compliant, detailed, organized, exacting, neat, careful, cautious, and a rule-follower. My wonderful husband, on the other hand, is 5 percent on the C-scale, which means naturally he is not detailed, but is arbitrary, unsystematic, colors outside the lines, likes to challenge status quo, and has many different ways of doing things. Let's just say, he doesn't care much for instructions or care to follow directions.

So I confess to you, I spent the first eleven years of our marriage being frustrated and many times mad at my husband. I expected him to think like I think and do things like I do. How hard is it anyway to put the round Tupperware inside of round ones and the square ones inside of the square ones and stack them neatly? To put things back where you got them from when you are done with them? To simply just be organized, neat, and detailed!

In my "aha" moment, for the first time ever, I realized that I needed to stop expecting my husband to be someone he was not created to be. He simply just isn't wired that way. Thankfully, because of what I have learned through TTI's DISC behaviors and Motivators, I am no longer frustrated. We actually have learned how to "meet in the middle" and I am learning how to let go. I thank God for the revelation he downloaded to me that day which changed everything and helped us to value each other even in our differences.

Now that we know what we know, the power of the DISC behaviors and Motivators language has helped us in so many ways, not only with each other, but in all our relationships. We even changed the way we parent our three children because we discovered how they are different and uniquely wired in their DISC behaviors and Motivators as well. We speak a new language that has helped us immensely and have become better at reminding each other of what we need because we are different. We even switched around some of our roles because of what we learned about each other. To demonstrate this, I will share stories throughout this book. What I am going to share with you has personally enhanced our marriage, our connection with our kids, and has changed how we do relationships! It is my prayer that it will help you and transform your relationships too.

As I have done debriefs of these assessments with couples over the years, I have had so many people say, "We wish we would have known this years ago. This would have saved us so much heartache and frustration. Every couple needs to know this about each other, and families as well." I absolutely love doing teambuilding workshops and couples, families, and individual debriefs along with career coaching. This book is a compilation of what people receive in my workshops and debriefs. Enjoy and be transformed!

Please note that I have used singular personal pronouns
in place of "they/them" in the text. To be fair,
I have alternated the use of he/she and him/her.

CHAPTER 1

THE POWER OF
DISC BEHAVIORS AND MOTIVATORS

He who knows others is learned.

He who knows himself is wise.

~ Lao Tse ~

I absolutely love it when people receive revelation from learning about DISC and Motivators. After one of the *Understanding Me, Understand You* classes I taught at Bethel Church, a couple came up to me and were so excited to share their testimony and new found revelations.

We have spent many years searching and attending a variety of different classes to help our marriage and we finally got our breakthrough! During the class, I received instant insight and understanding into why I do what I do and why my husband responds the way he does. That simple understanding of how we respond differently due to our innate behavior styles changed everything for us. For the first time ever, we see beyond each other's natural responses to the heart. Now my husband understands that my heart's intent is to help, not to hurt. A big shift took place from constantly misunderstanding each other to one of newly found understanding through learning about each other, how we respond, and how we are wired.

~ Jazelle and Gary ~

Throughout this book I'm going to introduce you to the two very powerful tools mentioned above. The DISC Behaviors Assessment reveals HOW you do what you do—it is your observable behaviors and emotions that you demonstrate. It is how you walk, talk, shop, drive, work, play—the language of people watching. The Motivators Assessment reveals the WHY you do what you do. A motivator is what you feel deep down inside, what fulfills you, brings satisfaction, excites and motivates you. It has to do with things you get jazzed about. These assessments are heavily used in large corporations and organizations all over the world for sales training, improving communication, job hiring, placement, leadership development, and performance improvement. My heart has always been to bring these assessments and information to the everyday person, especially to couples, families, teams, non-profits, and ministries so they can also have access to this powerful information and experience the many benefits as well.

The list is much longer, but I would like to highlight a few of the benefits to learning about yourself and others. Knowing yourself, your DISC Behaviors and Motivators will help you in:

- relationships
- communication
- heart-to-heart connections
- understanding of others
- understanding of yourself
- self-awareness and personal development
- job satisfaction in finding your "sweet spot"
- conflict resolution
- understanding your differences

To get started on your DISCovery journey, you can simply read through this book to gain a basic understanding or you can go to www.betterconnections.net to purchase a reasonably priced DISC and/or Motivators assessment that best fits your current role in life.

In a nutshell, using DISC Behaviors Assessment is much like speaking foreign languages. An example of this is: if I speak Spanish and my husband, co-worker, or friend speaks French, and they do not know any Spanish, and I keep coming at them in Spanish all day long, how well are we going to get along and communicate? Not very well. This is a picture of what is taking place in many of our relationships and we don't even know it. This is why it is really important for us to learn each other's DISC Behavior language and what truly motivates. Understanding yourself and others is the first step to enhancing your relationships and developing effective communication. In addition, it is absolutely crucial that we learn how to adjust and ADAPT to one another as well. Repeat after me:

It's all about my approach.
I must ADAPT and change my approach to have
better connections, communication, relationships,
and it all starts with me!

The DISC Behaviors and Motivators Assessments are powerful tools, but they must be handled very carefully. This is never an excuse to continue on in any negative behavior or say, "This is who I am, deal with it!" NO. Please do not ever misuse the tools in this way. We all have the ability to adapt to one another. The whole purpose of these tools is to understand each other and to adapt to one another, so you can begin to speak each other's language.

Our goal is NOT to LABEL, but to UNDERSTAND
and to know how to APPROACH each other for a WIN-WIN.

In this book, I am handing you a key that is chocked full of information that has the power and potential to radically transform your relationships. However, it will not do you any good to leave it laying on your table. You must pick up the key and use it. Keep it at the forefront of your mind in order for this to transform your relationships. Why? Because information does not produce transformation; doing something with it does! You hold the key in your hand. So now it's up to you. Start with the end in mind. What will you do with everything you learn from this book and how will you apply it to your life and your relationships for transformation?

Also, please keep in mind as you learn about the different DISC Behavior styles, this is not meant to put people in a box. Its purpose is to help you communicate and understand others better so that you can honor and celebrate each other even more. I could take fifty people who show up a certain way in the DISC Behaviors profile and not one of them will be like the others, because each person is unique in so many ways. Each person has different characteristics coming into play which color their behavior styles differently. That's why I always want to bring in as much as I can because everyone is unique and multifaceted.

When I debrief someone, I like to look at their Motivators, DISC Behaviors, Strengths, Emotional Quotient, Hard and Soft Skills, Spiritual Gifts, and Love Languages. The more we see, the more they can know and discover about themselves. This aids in giving them a clearer picture of what they truly need to thrive and what environments are best for them along with how to better communicate and understand others. These assessments are also essential in career coaching to help people discover what they were truly created for and to guide them to a place where they are "thriving" not just "surviving."

In my research I came across these riveting statistics by The Barna Group of Ventura, California (www.barna.org).[1] Did you know that feeling misunderstood is one of the most widespread and long-lasting difficulties felt by most young people? The Barna Group found of the thirteen issues posed to parents, some of the most pressing issues for teenagers that were somewhat to very significant are:

45 percent – not having enough money

43 percent – feeling misunderstood by their family

40 percent – struggling with their self-image

37 percent – not owning the latest technology

33 percent – not wearing the "right" clothing

For those younger than thirteen, by far the most serious issues were:

41 percent – feeling misunderstood by their family

32 percent – being made fun of by their peers

26 percent – struggling with their self-image

26 percent – not feeling accepted by their peers

© The Barna Group, Ltd, 2009[1]

I found this shocking that close to half of the young people in both groups are profoundly affected by feeling misunderstood by their families and that this runs deeper than even self-image or being accepted by their peers. WOW!

In response to this, my heart and the purpose of this book are right there! I want to help everyone in relationships have a new understanding and revelation for yourself, your spouse, your kids, and those you do life with. I want to give you practical ways to implement the information in this book so that it creates transformation in all your relationships—so you can have better connections. My prayer is that this book will do just that.

In addition to this book, to increase your understanding and to identify the many different facets of your original design, there are a myriad of different assessments you can take:

- MOTIVATORS: Learn WHY you do what you do, what you care about most, what motivates you and doesn't motivate someone else. This is absolutely essential for finding your "sweet spot" or a career that fulfills and energizes you.

- DISC BEHAVIORS: Learn HOW you do what you do, understand your observable behaviors and those of others you interact with.

There are a variety of DISC assessments to choose from depending on your role in life and dependent on what you want to learn:

~ Family Relationships DISC for families

~ Excellence for Learning DISC for students and teachers

~ Talent Insights DISC and Motivators for everyone, couples, students, teams, and career coaching

~ Management Staff DISC for managers

Dependent on what you want to discover, the other types of Assessments available:

• EMOTIONAL QUOTIENT: Discover how you handle your various emotions internally and externally with others

• PTSI OR DNA INSIGHTS: What you do WELL, your talents, abilities, hard and soft skills

• BLUEPRINT FOR LIFE (an add-on to the assessments)[3]: Discover WHAT you were created to be and do for God, your unique purpose, destiny, calling for greater fulfillment

If you're interested in any of the assessments above, would like to have a personal debrief, host a workshop in your church or organization, or want to become DISC and Motivators certified, for more information please go to: WWW.BETTERCONNECTIONS.NET

CHAPTER 2

ONE BODY, MANY PARTS

The way God designed our bodies is a model
for understanding our lives together as a church:
every part dependent on every other part, the parts we mention
and the parts we don't, the parts we see and the parts we don't.
If one part hurts, every other part is involved in the hurt,
and in the healing. If one part flourishes,
every other part enters into the exuberance.

1 Corinthians 12:25-26 (MSG)

I wonder what the world would look like if we all appreciated and celebrated those who are different from us, valuing uniqueness of what each person brings to the kingdom. I love how God is so creative, yet so intentional about forming the body of Christ. Eugene H. Peterson describes this so well in his version of 1 Corinthians 12:12-18:

You can easily enough see how this kind of thing works by looking no further than your own body. Your body has many parts—limbs, organs, cells—but no matter how many parts you can name, you're still one body. It's exactly the same with Christ. By means of his one Spirit, we all said good-bye to our partial and piecemeal lives. We each used to independently call our own shots, but then we entered into a large and integrated life in which he has the final say in everything. (This is what we proclaimed in word and action when we were baptized.) Each of us is now a part of his resurrection body, refreshed and sustained at one fountain—his Spirit—where we all come to drink. The old labels we once used to identify ourselves—labels like Jew or Greek, slave or free—are no longer useful. We need something larger, more comprehensive.

I want you to think about how all this makes you more significant, not less. A body isn't just a single part blown up into something huge. It's all the different-but-similar parts arranged and functioning together. If Foot said, "I'm not elegant like Hand, embellished with rings; I guess I don't belong to this body," would that make it so? If Ear said, "I'm not beautiful like Eye, limpid and expressive; I don't deserve a place on the head," would you want to remove it from the body? If the body was all eye, how could it hear? If all ear, how could it smell? As it is, we see that God has carefully placed each part of the body right where he wanted it.

But I also want you to think about how this keeps your significance from getting blown up into self-importance. For no matter how significant you are, it is only because of what you are a part of. An enormous eye or a gigantic hand wouldn't be a body, but a monster. What we have is one body with many parts, each its proper size and in its proper place. No part is important on its own. Can you imagine Eye telling Hand, "Get lost; I don't need you"? Or, Head telling Foot, "You're fired; your job has been phased out"? As a matter of fact, in practice it works the other way—the "lower" the part, the more basic, and therefore necessary. You can live without an eye, for instance, but not without a stomach. When it's a part of your own body you are concerned with, it makes no difference whether the part is visible or clothed, higher or lower. You give it dignity and honor just as it is, without comparisons. If anything, you have more concern for the lower parts than the higher. If you had to choose, wouldn't you prefer good digestion to full-bodied hair?

The way God designed our bodies is a model for understanding our lives together as a church: every part dependent on every other part, the parts we mention and the parts we don't, the parts we see and the parts we don't. If one part hurts, every other part is involved in the hurt, and in the healing. If one part flourishes, every other part enters into the exuberance.[1]

You are Christ's body—that's who you are! You must never forget this. Only as you accept your part of that body does your "part" mean anything. [1]

All needed. All unique. What a powerful demonstration we would be for the kingdom of God if every person stepped into his or her God-given original design. We don't need you to be different by conforming to the world; the kingdom needs you to be you. God's orignal intent in creating us so differently is so that we can complete each other, not to compete with each other! You bring to the table what I don't have. I need you and what you bring. We need all the parts of the body to be activated. As the body of Christ, we need to get better at celebrating each other and our differences.

You are so incredibly multifaceted and unique there is so much that makes you who you are: natural talents, core values, spiritual gifts, personality traits, strengths, internal motivators, skills and abilities, behavior styles, passions, and simply your life experiences to name a few. God has designed you with intention and purpose. You are his original design created for God-given assignments reserved just for you. So before we jump into the details of DISC an Motivators, I believe it is really important to first look at yourself and others through Heaven's perspective, because you are fearfully and wonderfully made. (Psalm 139:14 NIV emphasis added)

HEAVENLY PERSONA AND EARTHLY PERSON

Excerpt from Graham Cooke's audio teaching,
Living Your Truest Identity[2]

*"How you see yourself is directly related to how you see God.
Who you perceive God is for you, shapes your personality,
your identity, your own self-awareness in the kingdom."*

~ Graham Cooke ~

In your multifacetedness you are also a combination of your "Heavenly Persona" and what I call your "Earthly Person." Much of what is written in this chapter is an excerpt from Graham Cooke's *True Identity* teaching. Throughout his teaching, Graham makes reference to "Personality," but I'm going to refer to this as your "Earthly Person," because I believe there is so much more to you than what the word "personality" defines.

When I do a personal debrief of someone's assessment, I am only looking at their "Earthly Person." I like to ask lots of questions because I really want to hear from that person and not just what the assessment might say. I also want to consider and hear who God says they are in their multifacetedness of their original design. Graham Cooke has a great example of this. He says, "When I go to conferences, people want me to show up in my Heavenly Persona, not my Earthly Person. Yet my family is not always wanting me showing up in my prophetic Heavenly Persona. They just want Graham."

Graham said something that has profoundly impacted me: "How you see yourself is directly related to how you see God." With that in mind, how do you see God? Unfortunately, most people have a distorted picture of God and haven't fully realized why Jesus came. Most believe Jesus came to pay for our sins, which is true. But he also came to restore the original picture which has suffered much damage over the years. Jesus came to demonstrate a loving God whose plan from the fall was to restore his family through Jesus's once-and-for-all love sacrifice. Jesus demonstrated an affectionate God who had come near. Jesus was on a mission to "show and tell" us who Father God is—to reveal Father God to us—to change our picture. Do you see God as a loving Father? Did you know that Jesus used the term "Father" to refer to God 149 times in the Gospels—37 times in Matthew, 5 times in Mark, 13 times in Luke, and 94 times in John? So, He's not just Jesus's Father, but our heavenly Father.[3]

In Genesis 2:7, in the very beginning we see God as the sculptor, the Master Artist, making man out of the ground. Then the Master Artist breathes into the art, giving it life so now all art reflects the Master Artist. Love is at His very core. Whether He leads us to green pastures, beside still waters, or is with us through the valley of the shadow of death, all His guidance in our lives comes from love. Whether He is protecting us, stretching us, molding or shaping us— all His interactions in our lives come from love.

So how does God see you? Do you believe He has to fix you or are you His canvas? Is He your solver or Savior? Is He fixing you or making you new? You are a fresh canvas on which God intends to paint you as His masterpiece.[4] He enjoys all his thoughts about you. He loves to tell you who you are. Are you listening? That is why we have prophecy—He gets to brag about you in public. He gets to open you up to, "This is how I see you." God loves to make beautiful things. Look at each one of us—so unique in so many ways, not one like the other, as intricate as a snowflake and individual as your fingerprint. You are His masterpiece—a work in progress. And when you are His that makes you royalty, sons and daughters of the Most High King, created in His own image, made to have dominion over all the earth, according to Genesis 1:26-28 (NIV). He sees not your history, but your destiny. Not what you are, but what you will become. God does not see like we do. We see a sinner, He sees the destined saint. He sees the masterpiece hidden under the mud. He sees what your life will become after being loved for a lifetime by Jesus.

The following is how Graham Cooke defines our God-given identity. Our God-given identity is made up of "who we are on earth" and "how we are known in heaven."

- Our EARTHLY PERSON is who we are on earth: soul, mind, body, psyche, intellect, emotions, physical attributes, behavioral styles, personality traits, experiences shaped by environment, upbringing, training, a learned behavior that can be either positive or negative.
- Our HEAVENLY PERSONA is how we are known and perceived in heaven: the specific persona in Jesus that you are designed to represent, carry, and reflect. It is a specific expression of God's image in you, how He wants to be seen in and through you.

When God gives us a specific assignment, He gives us elevated status, everything we need to do what we do best. When we align with heaven and step into your Heavenly Persona, all favor, permission, provision, and legal authority is in that place. In that place is where we are highly favored—perceived perpetually in God.

YOUR HEAVENLY PERSONA IS:
- How God sees you, NOT how you see yourself
- Your charge from heaven in which purpose is formed
- The role you adopt as you learn how to be and do, behave and become

Your Heavenly Persona is the role you adopt for yourself. You put on Christ. You put Him on specifically in the area He's designed you to be—your destiny. In your Heavenly Persona, you have legal authority and charge over that specific calling of your life. You have a particular charge from heaven. What would the kingdom look like if everyone stepped into their Heavenly Persona and we were all better at calling it forth in others as well? If only we celebrated each other like God celebrates each one of us!

Now some of you are asking, "How do I discover my Heavenly Persona?" Here's how:

- GOD FIRST – Go to God first, discover and get to know "who you are" and what you've got permission, authority, and favor for.
- WORDS – What prophetic words have been spoken over you? What have others said? What are your spiritual gifts?
- SCRIPTURES – What has God spoken to you personally? What Scriptures have grabbed your heart? What are your inheritance words? Which Scriptures identify who you are?
- CHARACTERISTICS – What specific characteristic of Jesus do you reflect to the world? What do you carry?
- ALIGNMENT – Come into alignment with that vision God has over you. You will have freedom to be and become.
- SEE AND BELIEVE – If you don't see or believe it, then you won't develop it. What do you see? Ask for God's eyes and heaven's perspective.
- LEARN – Learn how to see, think, behave, speak, align, and walk in your Heavenly Persona.
- PRACTICE – Begin to practice your permissions. The body of Christ needs you to be you.

Graham goes on to explain that when we step into our Heavenly Persona, because of the love of God, we will experience some negative things from our Earthly Person emerging to the surface. Initially we make excuses because we are undeveloped in our Earthly Person. But God, the Master Artist, puts us on the potter's wheel to mold and shape us, ridding us of the negative parts of our Earthly Person. God is always more concerned about our character than he is with our comfort. Yet God, in His loving kindness and goodness wants to get rid of anything that hinders us or keeps us from walking in the fullness of our destiny. He will always speak to you as to whom you are becoming. Interestingly enough, what we behold is what we become. What are you beholding?

There are examples of negative things bubbling up in people all throughout the Bible. Do you remember what Moses did when he encountered God at the burning bush? I'll paraphrase: "What? Not me. Send someone else. I have a-a-a-a-a stutter. I can't speak." That was Moses's negative stuff coming to the surface. But God says, "Nevertheless, no problem. You're going and you can deliver my people. I'll be with you!"

Another example is in Judges 6:12-16, when God addresses Gideon and speaks to his Heavenly Persona not his Earthly one:

> The angel of the Lord appeared to him and said to him, "The Lord is with you, O valiant warrior." Then Gideon said to him, "O my lord, if the Lord is with us, why then has all this happened to us? And where are all His miracles which our fathers told us about, saying, 'Did not the Lord bring us up from Egypt?' But now the Lord has abandoned us and given us into the hand of Midian."

> The Lord looked at him and said, "Go in this your strength and deliver Israel from the hand of Midian. Have I not sent you?" He said to Him, "O Lord, how shall I deliver Israel? Behold, my family is the least

in Manasseh, and I am the youngest in my father's house." But the Lord said to him, "Surely I will be with you, and you shall defeat Midian as one man." (NASB)

God isn't interested in how you feel on earth, but how you are perceived in heaven—elevated status, legal authority over the enemy, permission to overcome. Gideon also responded out of his Earthly Person. And once again, God responded, "Nevertheless!! I'll be with you. You didn't see yourself as a mighty warrior, but you are now."

Other Examples:

	EARTHLY PERSON	HEAVENLY PERSONA
David	Shepherd, Adulterer	King, Man after God
Abraham	Childless	Father of many nations
Moses	Murderer, Shepherd	Deliverer of Israel
Mary	Teenage servant girl	Mother of Jesus

God will never answer you in your Earthly Persona. He will be with you to develop your Heavenly Persona. He talks to you from that place. You get to deal with your inadequacies as stepping stones to engage with God and the Holy Spirit. You are in training for reigning and learning about whom He says you are. You are learning to pray from a different place. God will reassure you in that place. You have the right and permission to pull down heaven into your circumstances. God wants you to be confident about who you are. Confident like David, because He already knew the outcome. You have to get your information from heaven. The whole point of prophecy is to open yourself up to your real identity. You need to discover who you are essentially and step into it. Your friends and family need to empower you to be you. Your Heavenly Persona is your permission to step into the fullness of God. Even in that, there is a battle going on between your Earthly Person and your Heavenly

Persona. The love of God will continue to challenge you because he wants to get rid of anything that hinders you or holds you back.

Everything in the Bible is yours. Step into it. Lay hold of it. You can have what it says. It is yours, claim it, grab onto it, and walk in it. Ask God, "What specific characteristic of who you are have you deposited in me to reflect back to the world? What do I carry and display?" This is who you are! And remember, call that forth in others as well. I love what Graham says, "If we don't see it, we won't develop it!" So, what are you seeing? What are you believing? Ask God, "Is there anything that I am believing that is keeping me from all that you have for me?" Let him show you and then get rid of the negative and walk in all that He has for you instead!

Believe it, see it, align with it, step into it, practice it!

You can find this entire teaching entitled
"Living your Truest Identity" by Graham Cooke at:
www.brilliantbookhouse.com/living-your-truest-identity
Adapted with permission from Graham Cooke.

CHAPTER 3

EARTHLY PERSON:
THE FACET OF MOTIVATORS

Next to physical survival, the greatest need of a human being
is psychological survival—to be understood, to be affirmed,
to be validated, to be appreciated.
~ Stephen Covey ~

Now that you have the foundation of your Heavenly Persona, you can begin to explore your God-given design and passions. One of the facets of your Earthly Person that I want to introduce you to is your Motivators which is: the WHY you do what you do—what satisfies you and fulfills you. Whereas the DISC facet is observable behavior—the HOW you do what you do.

Motivators are so important! To the extent that today's corporations are looking to develop the potential of each individual, realizing that a healthy, motivated work force leads to a healthy, profitable company. Special attention is now focused on the "fit of the person with the job." Each individual is unique just as each career is unique. If the individual is matched to the appropriate career, success should follow.

Studies suggest that over 50 percent of the work force may be in jobs that are not suited to who they are and what they value. A study from California suggests the number is as high as 90 percent. The cost of hiring a person who is a "misfit" to the job can be as high as ten times their annual salary. Companies all over the world are realizing that an investment on pre-selection assessments can facilitate a win-win scenario for the employee and the company, moving both toward their goals and redirecting others to a position where a win-win is achievable. So if you know your Motivators and your career is an extension of who you are, you will not have to be motivated. You will get up in the morning and desire to go to work because your environment will be providing the "valuing or motivation" you need in order to achieve your maximum potential.

For example:
- If you value knowledge and the search for truth, how will you survive and grow in a career that doesn't challenge your learning or allow for continuing education? (Theo)
- If you value form, harmony, beauty, and balance, how will you grow in an environment that is chaotic and un-balanced? (Aesthetic)
- If you live by a closed system of principles, will you grow in a company that actively promotes an opposing system of beliefs to yours? (Traditional)
- If you have a passion to lead, direct, and impact others, wouldn't you be more fulfilled in a career that allows for quick advancement and place where you can make that kind of impact? (Individualistic)
- If you have a heart for helping people, and are in an environment where you are not able to help others, would you thrive? (Social)

- On the contrary, if you are in an environment that has established rewards for your return on investment of time, talent, and resources, would you be thriving? (Utilitarian)[1]

Motivators are so important that you want to spend 80 percent of your day in your top two. And yes, the Motivators Assessment can quickly help you to identify what that is for you. Motivators wraps language around that which you probably already know about yourself, but now it is clearly expressed and validated. These are valuable because they are essential for career coaching, team-building, communication, and training and are being utilized in organizations all over the world to enhance understanding and potential.

Motivators were developed from Eduard Spranger's work in which he observed six attitudes through which we value the world. These attitudes define the "why" of your actions. You move into these based on what you value—what motivates you, pursuing that which you value. You will tend to be negative or indifferent toward experiences and people whose "valuing" is opposite of yours. Of the six attitudes observed by Spranger, your understanding and application of your top two Motivators will move you quickly into action towards the achievement of your potential. Motivators identify six attitudes, dimensions or world views, examines the passions that lead us to action, and the "WHY" of our actions.

The six dimensions evaluated include Theoretical (Theo), Utilitarian (Util), Aesthetic (Aes), Social (Soc), Individualistic (Ind), and Traditional (Trad). Your scores reflect what motivates you and what doesn't. In a debrief we look at the top two, middle two, and lowest two. When I'm debriefing a person, many times I consider the third and fourth Motivator as well to see how it may be playing out in his or her life situation, especially if either one shows up as passionate in the "Norms and Comparisons" chart which I will explain at the end of this chapter.

It is important to learn about all six categories because you do life with all six types that show up in the variety of people you interact with at home, work or play. When I debrief Motivators with couples and teams, great understanding comes and the light bulbs go on. This is such a beautiful thing! The "ah ha" expressed is, "Now I understand why we're so different!" Motivators bring understanding into what is going on between people who are motivated by many different things.

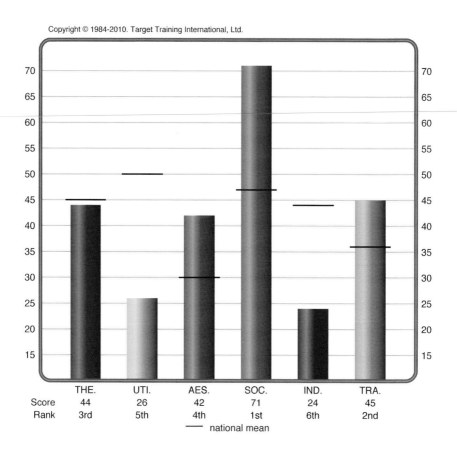

	THE.	UTI.	AES.	SOC.	IND.	TRA.
Score	44	26	42	71	24	45
Rank	3rd	5th	4th	1st	6th	2nd

— national mean

So Where Exactly Do Motivators Come From?

Every day we are faced with real situations that call for thought, decision, opinion, and action. Consciously or subconsciously, every decision, reaction, and course of action arises from our beliefs, our values, and our attitudes which TTI defines as our Motivators. It is said by some that we are the sum total of all of our experiences. Multiple experiences lead to beliefs. The intensity of each experience results in beliefs of varying strengths. The repetition of the same experiences also strengthens the beliefs into our Motivators. Motivators are what drives a person and conversely, Motivator scores can also indicate drivers to which a person may be indifferent. With Motivators, we can make informed assumptions about what a person wants to spend his or her time and energy on.

Experiences ⇨ Beliefs ⇨ Values = Motivators

Remember with a person's Motivators, there is no good or bad. We all value things differently. However, if an individual is placed in an environment that satisfies his top two or three motivators, the chance for success greatly increases. Motivators are more accurately defined as "that which you value." Your experiences lead to beliefs which cluster together into your values (that which motivates you). Conversely, your beliefs will also cluster together into that which you do not value. Your valuing of life then shapes itself over time into your worldview.

Defining the Six Different Motivators

Theoretical

Let's start with the high Theoretical. They love, love, love, love knowledge and learning, and they want to know how everything works. They are very objective. They do not take anything at face value. If one plus two equals three, how did you get there? What does that look like? Where's the validity behind that? They just love that stuff. High Theoreticals are problem solvers. They are very objective and identify truths and untruths. Those who score high Theoretical tend to be professors, researchers, scientists, and the type of person who has all those letters behind their name. They may have a PhD, their masters, or doctorates because they are lifelong learners and have the tendency to become experts in their areas of passion.

Each one of these has a shadow side that has to be managed. A perfect picture of someone who is high Theoretical that has entered the shadow side and is out of balance would be the mad scientist in his lab. He's not brushing his teeth, showering, combing his hair, or paying the bills, and is not going to come out until he's gained as much knowledge and wisdom possible in order to finish the job. There are different ways the Theoretical can play out in someone's life. There's the history buff who is like a walking Trivial Pursuit. Some Theoreticals tell you all kinds of interesting facts that you normally would not know while others take all they learned and apply it to the future.

UTILITARIAN

People who score high in Utilitarian love to see the return on their investment of their time, talent, and resources. Utilitarians are practical in all areas of life. They utilize resources effectively. It is important for Utilitarians to see measurable results and change. It seems as though, they have filters in their brains where they are evaluating everything they see. They ask themselves, "Is this worth my time, my talent, and resources?" If it's not, there will be no signing up and he will move on. Utilitarians tend to be in sales because there are rewards, incentive programs, and measurement of results. Also, the Utilitarian thrives in the area of finance, consulting, organizational development, or wellness—because anything that is results driven or is a short-term project where the Utilitarian can see the results is a motivation factor. Measureable results are really important for the Utilitarian to feel satisfied. They have to be careful not to miss opportunities because they evaluated the opportunity too quickly and disqualified it. Also when it comes to people, they have a tendency to focus on the product, end results, or the sale. This can also make them very driven, going from one accomplishment to the next, not taking the time to celebrate their progress.

AESTHETIC

Aesthetics exist to experience harmony, beauty, peace with all the senses. Aesthetics are creative and expressive people. They tend to understand the feelings of themselves and others. They are very appreciative of everything around them—their environment, nature, and their surroundings. Some Aesthetics are very sensitively wired. What I mean by that is when they walk into a room and see there is tension, they pick up on it and it can actually become physically upsetting to them. It's so strong for some Aesthetics that they have to leave and cannot stay in that place. Environment and being able to creatively express themselves is everything to the Aesthetic.

Have you ever been in a large corporate office where there are rows and rows of cubicles? If you walked up and down those aisles, you would be able to identify the Aesthetic's cubicle immediately. How? Inside that cubicle is an environment that they have created in order to thrive. There would be paintings on the wall, green plants, lamps with just the right lighting, probably soft music playing, lots of color, and a rug. It would be coordinated beautifully. This is necessary for the Aesthetic because they have to have beautiful, harmonious environments in which to dwell.

Now let me clarify—this is where it can get really interesting. Some people are just naturally gifted and talented in specific areas, such as interior design for example. They are naturally good at it, but it does not mean that they are highly Aesthetic. The key factor here is whether or not they can live without it. For most Aesthetics, they would not be okay. But for someone who is just gifted naturally in interior design, she can dwell in any environment. Make sense?

I will use myself as an example. By trade, I have been a graphic designer for over twenty-five years. It is a natural talent and gift I have. However, it doesn't fulfill me or bring me satisfaction. When I took the Motivators Assessment, I found out that my fulfillment comes from helping people and making a big impact in people's lives. After that discovery, I switched careers. Now I absolutely love what I do as a life coach and trainer because it is all about helping people and transforming lives! You know you are in touch with passion and fulfillment when that is all you want to do. It is even more beautiful when you get paid for it. Remember when I said that you want to be in your top two motivators at least 80 percent of your day, so that you are feeling satisfied and fulfilled most of the time? How many people have you met that can truly say, "I absolutely love what I do?" Before, as a graphic designer, yes, maybe I helped a little, but pretty much everything I did eventually ended up in the trash. That was not very impactful or very satisfying for me at all. It was just a job that helped pay the bills. There is a big difference in my fulfillment between what I used to do and what I do now.

SOCIAL

People who score high in Social exist to help other people achieve their potential. They are developers of others, champions of worthy causes, and they are generous with their time, talents, and resources. Most people who score high in Social tend to be in the helping professions such as: Social services, counseling, coaching, education, ministry, missions, nonprofits, human resources, etc. This can play out as mission, world saving, or just giving to others in your immediate sphere of influence.

INDIVIDUALISTIC

People who score high in Individualistic exist to make a big impact. They will successfully achieve and utilize their position and power. They are leaders, they form alliances, they plan and carry out winning strategies, and they accomplish purposes. It is no surprise that high Individualistics end up being presidents, governors, senators, congressmen, mayors, CEOs, and CFOs. They thrive in positions which can impact a larger mass of people. The bottom line is they need a platform or a position from which they can impact the masses. The Individualistic can play out in many different ways. They can have a drive for destiny of self or destiny of others. The high Individualistics do have to be careful when they are leading as to not come across too assertive, threatening, neglecting others, or taking on too much, which could end up in loss of opportunity.

TRADITIONAL

High Traditionals exist to pursue a meaningful or divine system of living. This one is a bit tougher to identify because I really need to sit down with people and ask them about their system of living. In this identified system they have a desire to understand totality of life; they will find meaning in that system of living; they will die for a cause; and they will live according to a closed book. Their desire is to convert others to live by that same system of living. For the Traditional there is a certain way of living and doing things and they want others to live the same way. Traditional used to be called "Religion." You could run someone's faith through the previous list to see it and understand how it plays out. If the system is not faith, instead it could play out my as a protector type system of living, an example of this could be the military.

Those who are high in Traditional need to understand that sometimes their specific system of living can come across as close-minded to other people who are non-Traditional. The non-traditional does not understand the self-sacrificing elements, and sometimes can feel like you are in opposition to their beliefs because a Traditional is not open or willing to try other systems of living. Traditional can play out on the reformer side of things or it can play out on the protector side of things.

To help you with this understanding of Motivators, let's use a shopping analogy. Everyone has different habits and buying styles. If we divide them into the six motivators, examples would be:

- Some people buy after thorough research (THEO).
- Some people buy to maximize their spending or saving (UTIL).
- Some people buy because they enjoy the look or feel (AES).
- Some people buy because it will help others (SOC).
- Some people buy because it will improve their status (IND).
- Some people buy because they've always bought the same way (TRAD).

We may do things that sound like one motivator; but if you dig deeper and ask WHY the person does something, you will see the connection to another motivator. Example: Some people who consider themselves stylish dressers actually have low Aesthetic scores. Aesthetic is a motivator that demonstrates value to the way things look and feel. However, the stylish dress could be explained because the person scores high in Individualistic and dresses to impress rather than for the look or feel.

MOTIVATORS IN RELATIONSHIPS

If you scored as a high Theoretical and your wife did not, husbands, don't be surprised when your wife checks out or glazes over at all your vast wisdom and knowledge. It is just something that they are not as interested in. So don't get upset with them if they lose interest much quickly because they are not Theoretical. My advice to you high Theoreticals is for you to actually create your own groups or find people who are high Theoretical so you can have discussion groups. In that group is where your high Theoretical will be valued and will thrive.

Remember, if you have a high Utilitarian in your family, don't be offended when he automatically evaluates what the purpose is. Then asks to see a return on his investment and doesn't want to waste time. He cares about things that you may not be interested in at all. Thus another area where you could be opposites. This is what we call a "clash of values." The high Aesthetics need to have a specific environment in which they can dwell and care about those things. While Socials were born to help people and will shrivel up and die if they don't get to. The Individualistics need their platform from which they can impact the masses. And people who are high in Traditional have a strong moral compass of how life should be lived and wonder why everybody else doesn't feel the same way they do.

In addition, it is beneficial to see how these blend together. The following are some examples of blending: Let's say we have a person who is a Social-Traditional-Utilitarian. And this Social-Traditional-Utilitarian is discipling someone. She is pouring into a young adult, investing in her, and walking with her. What happens if this person that is being poured into and invested in comes back week after week and nothing has changed—she has taken no steps at all to move forward? I asked those who scored high in Utilitarian, "How does that make you feel?" Every time the Utilitarian's response is "Very frustrated. I feel like we're not getting anywhere, like we are wasting time." Utilitarians tend to reach a point where it is time to love 'em and leave 'em because they are not seeing any results or change.

I also have the privilege of training life coaches who use these tools, and if I see a coach with the Utilitarian factor in his top two, I always encourage him to watch that Utilitarian factor because, "Whose agenda is it? Their's or the person they are coaching?" So, if you had a different blend of Motivators with that same young adult being discipled, say a Social-Traditional-Aesthetic, this person would stay with the young adult for a much longer period of time. Why? Because it's not about the return on investment that is the motivating factor, instead it's about how the one being discipled is feeling.

One more example: A Social-Traditional-Individualistic—could be a pastor of a megachurch. Why? Because he exists to help people find the system of living which is his faith (TRAD) and will impact the masses from the platform (IND), because he has helped people through his message and teaching (SOC).

NORMS AND COMPARISONS

When you are with others who share your similar Motivators, you will find you have similar interests, will fit in with the group, and be energized. Those with Motivators significantly different from yours couldn't be more different and you may be perceived as out of the mainstream. When Motivators differ significantly, this can induce stress or conflict between two people.

You can see this much better by viewing your *Norms and Comparison* chart (found near page 30 in your assessment). The bar is what I like to call "the crowd" which represents 68 percent of the population. Sometimes you score outside the crowd on either side.

- The further from mainstream or the crowd your star is on the high (RIGHT) side, the more people will notice your passion about that Motivator.
- The further away from the mainstream or the crowd on the low (LEFT) side, the more people will view you as indifferent or that you really just don't care much about that particular motivator.

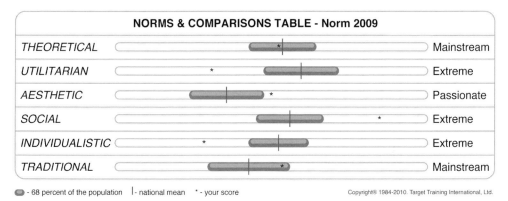

NORMS & COMPARISONS TABLE - Norm 2009

THEORETICAL	Mainstream
UTILITARIAN	Extreme
AESTHETIC	Passionate
SOCIAL	Extreme
INDIVIDUALISTIC	Extreme
TRADITIONAL	Mainstream

- 68 percent of the population | - national mean * - your score   Copyright® 1984-2010. Target Training International, Ltd.

Mainstream - one standard deviation of the national mean
Passionate - two standard deviations above the national mean
Indifferent - two standard deviations below the national mean
Extreme - three standard deviations from the national mean

As you can see, there are great benefits to knowing yourself, taking the assessments, and having a personal debrief—to sit down and go through this self-discovery process with a coach. A coach specializing in these assessments can help you to understand your blending. When you discover what truly fulfills and satisfies you, then you can be intentional about keeping that in the forefront as you move forward and operate in your top two motivators 80 percent of the time.

CHAPTER 4

DISC OVERVIEW: FLYING AT 60,000

It's not what style you are,
it's what you do with what you are.

~ Bill J. Bonnstetter ~

$\mathcal{N}$ext we will look at the facet of your DISC Behaviors. The "how" you do what you do. Keep in mind, there are a variety of different assessments available online today, but it is important you understand what the assessment is measuring. Also, I would highly recommend you only consider assessments that have been scientifically researched and validated for accuracy. So that you are receiving valid information about yourself in the discovery process. Please know that DISC Behaviors and Motivators are not personality tests. DISC only measures observable behaviors and emotions. This is simply HOW you walk, talk, shop, drive, work, play. How you respond to specific situations. How you approach life, right down to the type of emails you send.

Once you learn the DISC language and begin to observe those around you, you can begin to recognize a person's DISC Behavior style by observing their tone of voice, body language, the words they speak, and their pace. When I do workshops I like to start out with this exercise that simply asks, "Which bird do you identify with the most?"

- THE EAGLES: Are quick, decisive, unafraid, like challenge, adventure, have great vision, know what they want and go after, fly at 60,000 feet, and tell it like it is.

- THE PARROTS: Are talkative, colorful, free spirits, expressive, social, like to be in the spot light, have lots of ideas, talk fast, love people and are sometimes very random.

- THE DOVES: Are friendly, soft-spoken, loyal, sensitive, accommodating, caring, planners, steady-eddies, like a relaxed pace, like things to stay the same, like to know what to expect, you can count on them, and have their routines.

- THE OWLS: Are thinkers, observers, wise, precise, knowledgeable, neat, organized, detailed, concrete sequential, like order and doing things in order, like to follow the rules and think you should too.

The animal usage adapted from *Taking Flight* with permission © 2010 Merrick Rosenberg and Daniel Silvert. All Rights reserved.[1]

This is a fun exercise because it gives an understanding of how we see ourselves and others in comparison to the D, I, S, and C. All are one type of animal, a bird, yet each species is uniquely different from the other in how they approach life, respond, and communicate.

Throughout history, research has consistently shown that behavioral characteristics can be grouped together into four styles.

More importantly, learning these different styles helps us to understand how people approach problems, people, pace, and procedures. The following is a overview of each behavior style flying at 60,000 feet.

UNDERSTANDING THE D-EAGLES IN OUR WORLD
D STANDS FOR DOMINANCE

The dominant director, the driver, the D
unconquerable, demanding, aggressive, free
brave, decisive, competitive, tough
up to the task, direct, sometimes rough!

Quick to the draw, flip with the lip
you'll get it direct, straight from the hip
they'll climb any mountain, nothing's too high
they aim to succeed at whatever they try!

Results are the focus, press on to new heights
along the way, expect a few fights
dont' take it personal, they just speak their mind
so pick up the pace, or get left behind!

You may smirk a little when you hear them rant
of all that they'll win, if their wish you grant
give them a challenge that's brave and bold
stand back and watch as they bring home the gold!

Randy Widrick ~ ©2011 Target Training International, Ltd.

The following are key qualities that best describe the 85-100 percent D-Eagles and why we need them in our lives. I will explain the percentages later on in this book, along with the blending of styles. Just keep in mind I am referring to a pure D, I, S, or C in the following descriptions.

OUR 85-100 PERCENT D-EAGLES ARE:

Decisive, brave, problem solvers, visionaries, pioneering, results-oriented, ambitious, big picture thinkers, delegators, directors, assertive, bold, adventuresome, innovative, change agents, confident, courageous, competitive, and take us places we normally would not go.

HOW TO RECOGNIZE THE D-EAGLES IN YOUR WORLD:

- TONE OF VOICE: strong, loud, confident, direct
- WORDS: challenging, rapid, commanding, blunt, debating
- BODY LANGUAGE: direct eye contact, leans forward, assertive, determined
- PACE: fast, abrupt
- FIRST EMOTION: frustration, anger
- KEY QUALITIES: leader, decisive, visionary, competitive, change agent, forerunner
- LOOKING FOR: results and significance

In their "tell it like it is" demeanor, I sometimes describe the D-Eagles as not having filters. This means what comes into the brain comes out of the mouth and it is not always "candy-coated," shall we say. D-Eagles like to give advice and share their opinions freely. They also love a good debate. You always know where you stand with a D because they have no problem telling you. The unfiltered thoughts and opinions are processed outside the body for the whole world to hear and experience.

Some of the other behavior styles can take some of these behavior traits personally. I know I did for many years, and I found myself distancing or protecting myself from the D-Eagles in my life because I was afraid of them and thought they could hurt me with the things that they would say. As humans in our Earthly Person, it is very easy for us to misunderstand each other and to be misunderstood. Understanding the DISC language completely changed the way I view those who are different from me. It gave me new understanding of each one and changed how I viewed people and interacted with them.

If there is one thing that is essential for you to know about the D-Eagles it is this: their hearts' intent is to never personally attack you, though it may feel like it sometimes. They are just debating the facts, not you personally. That one statement has personally brought me so much freedom. I now can recognize someone's "D-ness" and remind myself, "Oh, don't take it personally, that's just their unadapted D coming at me." I understand now and don't have to be hurt or afraid of their D-ness. I love what Danny Silk says, "We need to get good at telling others what we need." So in this, it's okay to tell the D-Eagles in your life, "It would really honor me and help us if you would approach me in a gentler tone of voice and give me some time to think and respond."

Remember, anger and frustration is the D's first emotion. So, if you are in that place with a D-Eagle where his frustration is oozing out, it's okay to tell him, "I'd be happy to talk with you when you can talk to me in a calmer way." Many times we don't even realize how we are affecting people with our tone, words, body language, or pace. Self-awareness is a beautiful thing. That is why a culture of honor is a permission-based authentic culture where I can remind you of what I need. When we can lovingly tell the truth, let each other know what we need, we have just set into motion healthy relationships and are creating awareness for those that we love and do life with.

WHAT YOU NEED TO KNOW ABOUT YOUR Ds:

D-EAGLES LIKE:

- To debate the facts. If you say it's white, they'll say it's black. They love a good debate
- Freedom from control, details, and supervision
- Change, variety, challenge, and adventure—if they don't have that they'll get bored and restless.
- To take charge, delegate, and see results—if no one is taking charge, they will.
- To dominate, get in your space or get in your face
- To process information at a very fast rate
- Make quick decisions
- To talk fast, walk fast, simply like things to move fast
- The bottom line and prefer the bullet points
- To have choices and know their options
- To control their own world and destiny
- To be heard and be able to express their viewpoints
- Not afraid to take risks and they like to win
- You to "be bright, be brief, be gone!"

D-EAGLES DON'T LIKE:

- To be controlled
- To be told what to do—let it be their idea
- Talking about things that aren't relevant
- Maintenance or routine work or doing things "the way we've always done them"
- Being touchy-feely or hugged unless they initiate it
- Care so much about the details, just the bottom line
- To look back, only forward
- When things are inefficient
- When things are moving too slowly

UNDERSTANDING THE I-PARROTS IN OUR WORLD
I STANDS FOR INFLUENCE

Influencer, expressive, sanguine, the I
life's full of hope, the limit's the sky
enthusiastic, fun, trusting, charming
confident, optimistic, popular, disarming.

Words smooth as cream as they talk to you
winning you over to their point of view
a sparkling eye, a smile that's bright
in the dark of the night, the I sees the light.

A people person with a need to be liked
inspiring the team to continue to fight
talking a lot while getting work done
don't worry a bit, work should be fun.

A joke or two, expect a high five
the high I adds humor, keeps things alive
turn them loose and watch what's done
the team is inspired to work as one.

Randy Widrick ~ ©2011 Target Training International, Ltd.

The following are the key qualities that best describe the 85-100 percent I-Parrot and why we so need them in our lives:

OUR 85-100 PERCENT I-PARROTS ARE:

Brainstormers, creative, expressive, influential, motivators, encouragers, inspiring, optimistic, warm, emotional, enthusiastic, problem solvers, persuasive, personable, demonstrative, sociable, light-hearted, team players, people persons, and could even sell ice cubes to an Eskimo.

HOW TO RECOGNIZE THE I-PARROTS IN YOUR WORLD:

- TONE OF VOICE: energized, rapid, friendly, loud
- WORDS: emotional, verbal processor, fun, sociable
- BODY LANGUAGE: expressive, smiles, multiple hand gestures, touches, hugs, energetic
- PACE: fast, random
- FIRST EMOTION: optimism, positivity
- KEY QUALITIES: brainstormer of ideas, networker, encourager, and motivater
- LOOKING FOR: an experience and for fun

The I-Parrots bring fun wherever they go. They too are "outside the body" processors, similar to the D-Eagle, but it comes out in an emotional, expressive, touchy-feely way. You always know how an I-Parrot feels because she wears her emotions on her sleeve and sometimes tells you more than you care to know. Your I-Parrots are the ones who while driving down the road, read all the signs out loud. They see things and tell what they see or pretty much process everything outside their bodies for the world to hear and know. Their conversations can be quite random at times and hard to follow, because they are all over the place in their thoughts and ideas. Speaking of ideas—they have lots of them and lots of words to go with it. Once your I-Parrot is finished "Ideating," or processing all their thoughts and ideas out loud, it's ok to ask them, "So, where did you land?" For the I-Parrot, it will be necessary to put things in writing, because they are so fully present in every experience that they don't remember what they talked about in the last conversation they had. Another tip is they are totally fine with reminder texts or voicemails. Your I-Parrots have lots of acquaintances and want to be liked by pretty much everyone and like to have fun while getting the job done.

WHAT YOU NEED TO KNOW ABOUT YOUR I-PARROTS

I-PARROTS LIKE:

- Lots of people interaction
- Fun, freedom, flexibility
- To be involved
- To talk and be listened to
- Freedom from control and detail
- To go with the flow
- Variety in their day
- Time for relating and socializing
- When you let them dream and let them process out loud
- When you ask for their opinions
- Group activities and parties, the more the merrier
- Receiving recognition and specific affirmations
- When you accept them for who they are
- When you provide ideas for implementing action

I-PARROTS DISLIKE:

- Being rejected
- Being boxed in
- Being legislated or controlled
- Facts and figures
- Being impersonal
- When things are moving too slowly
- Setting goals or planning too far in advance
- Being overlooked
- Being muffled or not being listened to

UNDERSTANDING THE S-DOVES IN OUR WORLD
S STANDS FOR STEADINESS

The steady relater, amiable, high S
mild, laid back, patient, no stress
stable, sincere, passive, serene
great listening skills, and "ace" on the team.

Hard at work behind the scenes
helping to do what's best for the team
others will tire, the S will finish
determined to stay till the task is finished.

Loyal, devoted, they'll be here awhile
jumping around just isn't their style
won't leave a job until it is over
finish it first, they're not a rover

Acutely aware of people's needs
responding to personal hurts on the team
although appearing slow in the jobs they do
when it comes to a team, the S is the "glue."

Randy Widrick ~ ©2011 Target Training International, Ltd.

The following are the key qualities that best describe the 85-100 percent S-Dove and why we need them in our lives:

OUR 85-100 PERCENT S-DOVE ARE:

Loyal, warm, friendly, relaxed, steady, dependable, patient, calm, consistent, reserved, predictable, persistent, sincere, empathetic, stabilizers, sacrificial, finishers, maintainers, planners, supporters, servants, team-oriented, and are great listeners.

HOW TO RECOGNIZE THE S-DOVES IN YOUR WORLD:
- TONE OF VOICE: soft-spoken, warm, steady
- WORDS: calm, methodical, quiet yet friendly, listens vs. talks
- BODY LANGUAGE: relaxed, small gestures, non-emotional
- PACE: slow, relaxed
- FIRST EMOTION: none, draw out
- KEY QUALITIES: faithful, loyal, team player, supportive
- LOOKING FOR: security and trust

What you need to know about the S-Doves in your world is that (unlike your Is and Ds), they process everything inside the body. In their "steady-eddieness," they are having emotions, you just can't see them. So remember to check in with them. Don't overlook them just because they are not talking, as they naturally don't give information freely. It has to be drawn out. There is a wealth of insight inside your S-Doves, so don't forget to ask for their input. They truly are the "glue" that holds things together and are happy to steadily work behind the scenes as long as they are valued and appreciated for the routine work that they do.

You know you have had an encounter with an S-Dove when you leave the conversation realizing you know nothing about them. If you don't ask, they won't tell. They are happy to keep the personal focus on you and your needs at the time. Not to say they don't have needs, they do. You just have to work harder at drawing their needs to the surface.

One thing you absolutely need to know about your S is—never rush an S! Just don't do it! It won't go well for you. If you want to foster trust and security with your S-Doves, make sure you give them plenty of advanced notice, time to think, respond, and adjust.

WHAT YOU NEED TO KNOW ABOUT YOUR Ss:

S-DOVES LIKE:

- To finish what they started before moving on to another project
- Advance notice and logical reasons for changing things
- To know what to expect
- To be asked and involved in the planning
- Time to think and respond
- To work on fewer projects
- To work at a slower pace
- Routines and routine work
- A planned-out schedule with downtime
- Time to adjust to change
- Stability, safety, and peace
- Relating to others on a personal level
- Long-lasting relationships with people they can trust
- To know they're needed and appreciated
- To be known and to know that you care
- Harmony in relationships at home and work
- Smaller groups and deeper relationships
- To maintain status quo
- To receive feedback

S-DOVES DISLIKE:

- Being rushed
- Conflict
- Unexpected changes
- Not knowing the plan or having a plan
- When things are unpredictable
- Being forced to respond quickly

- Making quick decisions
- When people are impersonal
- Being taken advantaged of
- Jumping from project to project or juggling multiple projects at the same time
- A fast pace or being overscheduled
- Empty promises
- Not having time to relate on a more personal level

UNDERSTANDING THE C-OWLS IN OUR WORLD
C STANDS FOR COMPLIANCE

Compliant, analytical, melancholic, the C
methodical, courteous, accurate as can be
restrained, diplomatic, mature, precise
exacting, systematic, those standards are nice.

Planning and organizing done to perfection
the smallest detail is no exception
consistently clear with objective thinking
give the team top-notch results without even blinking.

And when it comes time to make a decision
you'd best have the facts to accomplish the vision
The C at your side with all correct facts
will assure the return on your investment won't lack.

Go by the book, follow the rules
procedures are written, use the right tools
standards are crucial, yet we need beta
in God we trust, still we value data!

Randy Widrick ~ ©2011 Target Training International, Ltd.

The following are the key qualities that best describe the 85-100 percent C-Owl and why we so need them in our lives:

Our 85-100 percent C-Owls Are:

Compliant, conventional, conscientious, courteous, organized, deliberate, detail-oriented, analytical, perfectionistic, systematic, diplomatic, knowledgeable, logical, concrete-sequential, precise, patient, reserved, objective, observers, task-oriented, concerned for quality, and they ask all the right questions.

How to Recognize the C-Owls in your world:

- Tone of Voice: monotone, precise, factual
- Words: observes, logical, inquiring, asks questions, concrete sequential
- Body Language: no gestures, controlled, stays distant
- Pace: slow and deliberate
- First Emotion: fear and doubt
- Key Qualities: detailed, organized, knowledgeable, accurate, concern for quality, and doing things right
- Looking for: information and details

What you need to know about the Cs in your world is that they also process everything inside their bodies. They too are having emotions and analyzing them, you just can't see them. Your Cs are observers. So don't be surprised when they do finally talk that they ask lots and lots of questions. Don't misunderstand the reason for their questions; they're simply gathering more information and details so they can do things really well. If the C-Owl doesn't have enough information or clear expectations and the task appears too vague or risky, don't expect them to sign up, because they won't. You must provide them with the information and expectations they need, so they can move forward with accuracy and quality.

Another thing to know about your C-Owls is that they need permission. Permission gives their compliant nature the confidence they need to move forward. Remember they're task-oriented and structured, they stick to business, are perfectionistic in nature, and they love crossing things off their lists. So if you walk into a C-Owl's office unannounced and feel like you are interrupting, you basically are. Because for the C, they receive great satisfaction in completing tasks and creating systems that effectively and seamlessly maintain themselves without interruption. When talking with a C, they too need time to think, research, analyze, and respond—so don't expect a quick response from them.

SO, WHAT YOU NEED TO KNOW ABOUT YOUR C-OWLS:

C-OWLS LIKE:

- Detailed information and data
- Time to think and respond
- Time to research and analyze information
- Clear expectations, preferably in writing
- To be informed and know what's happening
- To be asked for their input
- To focus on tasks and finish what they started with excellence
- Rules and procedures to follow
- When there is a concern for quality
- Reassurance, approval, and validation that they're doing things correctly or meeting expectations
- Fewer people interactions and small groups
- Being a part of a team, yet working individually on their own projects
- An office with a door or time to work or be alone

C-Owls Like: *(continued)*

- To set goals and reach them
- High standards and prefer others who value those too
- Their personal space

C-Owls Dislike:

- Making mistakes
- When their questions aren't answered
- To think, act, or decide quickly
- Unrealistic expectations
- When they don't have permission or approval
- When things are chaotic or noisy
- Disorganization, clutter, or disorder
- When they don't have time to do their research or time to do things well with quality and excellence
- To settle when there could be a better way
- When there's no concern for quality
- When things are vague or facts are missing
- Having to do things twice
- When they can't explore or research all their possible options
- Being rushed in their decision-making
- When people don't do what they said they would do
- When they can't finish the tasks they started
- When people overpromise
- Being touched unless they initiate it
- Sudden or abrupt changes

CHAPTER 5

THE EIGHT DIFFERENT SIDES OF DISC

Seek first to understand, and then to be understood.
~ Stephen Covey ~

As we begin to dig deeper, you will discover there is more than just four sides to DISC behaviors. There are actually eight different responses or sides. Everyone will score somewhere in each category of the D, I, S, and C on a 0 percent to 100 percent scale. Each category of DISC measures a different thing—from how you handle problems and challenges, to people, to pace of life, and how you handle rules and procedures set by someone else. It aids us in the understanding of predictable responses that occur for us as Earthly Persons to the same situation.

In the TTI DISC Assessment, the *Descriptors* (near p.10 of your assessment) shows these eight different sides of the DISC behaviors. In this chapter, I will explain the context of each side. The best way is to turn the page horizontally and add the labels which I added to each column, along with the percentages as shown below.

DESCRIPTORS

Based on the responses, the report has marked those words that describe personal behavior. They describe how you solve problems and meets challenges, influence people, respond to the pace of the environment and how you respond to rules and procedures set by others.

Dominance			Influencing			Steadiness			Compliance		
Demanding	Infielders	Assertive	Effusive	Optimistic	Flys at 60,000 Ft	Phlegmatic	Planner	Predictable/Slower	Evasive	Rule Follower	One Way/Structured
Egocentric			Inspiring			Relaxed			Worrisome		
Driving			Magnetic			Resistant to Change			Careful		
Ambitious			Political			Nondemonstrative			Dependent		
Pioneering			Enthusiastic						Cautious		
Strong-illed			Demonstrative			Passive			Conventional		
Forceful			Persuasive						Exacting		
Determined			Warm			Patient			Neat		
Aggressive			Convincing								
Competitive			Polished			Possessive			Systematic		
Decisive			Poised						Diplomatic		
Venturesome			Optimistic			Predictable			Accurate		
						Consistent			Tactful		
						Deliberate					
Inquisitive			Trusting			Steady			Open-Minded		
Responsible			Sociable			Stable			Balanced Judgement		
Conservative		Accommodating	Reflective	Realistic	On the Ground	Mobile	Spontaneous	Dynamic/Faster	Firm	Risk Taker	Pioneering/Many Ways
Calculating	Outfielders		Factual			Active			Independent		
Cooperative			Calculating			Restless			Self-Willed		
Hesitant			Skeptical			Alert			Stubborn		
Low-Keyed						Variety-Oriented					
Unsure			Logical			Demonstrative			Obstinate		
Undemanding			Undemonstrative								
Cautious			Suspicious			Impatient			Opinionated		
			Matter-of-Fact			Pressure-Oriented			Unsystematic		
Mild			Incisive			Eager			Self-Righteous		
Agreeable						Flexible			Uninhibited		
Modest			Pessimistic			Impulsive			Arbitrary		
Peaceful			Moody			Impetuous			Unbending		
Unobtrusive			Critical			Hypertense			Careless with Details		

100% — 50% — 0% (left scale)
100% — 50% — 0% (right scale)

D How you handle PROBLEMS & CHALLENGES

I INFLUENCE PEOPLE & IDEAS

S How you handle PACE OF LIFE & CHANGE

C RULES & PROCEDURES SET BY OTHERS

Wendy Crawford - TTI Value Added Associate
www.betterconnections.net

DEFINING THE D-SCALE = DOMINANCE

For starters, when defining the D-scale, I love to use the analogy of baseball. Why? Because on a baseball team there are two groups of people on the same team that are necessary to successfully play the game. You have your Infielders and your Outfielders. When we look at the D-Scale, we must consider the context and what the D-scale is actually measuring since we all score somewhere from 0 percent-100 percent on each scale of the D, I, S, and C.

It is very helpful and beneficial to know your percentage which you can find near page 20 in your Assessment. The percentages are located underneath your Natural Graph (the graph on the right). This helps you and others understand your natural response when it comes to life's various situations.

Copyright © 2012. Target Training International, Ltd.

THE D-SCALE IS HOW YOU PERSONALLY HANDLE PROBLEMS, CRISES, AND CHALLENGES

So let's say the ball in this picture is a problem, a challenge, a crisis coming at an Infielder. How would the Infielder naturally respond? Infielders are quick and decisive, and they attack the problem or challenge, catch the ball, make the play.

So let's consider the same ball, same problem,

same challenge coming at the Outfielder. How do they naturally respond? Totally different from that of the Infielder. Outfielders can take their time, position themselves, calculate, do their research, catch the ball, and still make the play. The point here is that both are absolutely needed on the team. One is not better than the other. Neither response is good or bad—just two different responses to the same situation, problem, challenge, or crisis coming at them.

With that context in mind, when it comes to a problem, a challenge, a crisis, or a big decision coming at you, how would you respond? Also think in terms of how your friend, co-worker, child, family member, or spouse would respond—the same or differently?

Let's take a closer look only at the D-scale from the *Descriptors* page. As you can see, a person who scores as a 5 percent on the D-scale would respond totally opposite than that of someone who scored as 100 percent on the same D-scale.

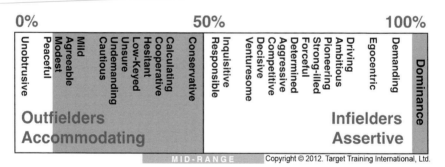

Now when you look at the words to the left and to the right of the middle line (50 percent line) they make much more sense in that context. The natural response of those who score 0-50 percent on the D-scale when it comes to problems, challenges, crises, and making big decisions are more: conservative, calculating, cooperative, hesitant, low-keyed, unsure, undemanding, cautious, mild, agreeable, modest, peaceful, unobtrusive. On the other hand those who score 50-100 percent on the D-scale, their responses will be more: venturesome, forceful, competitive, aggressive, determined, strong-willed, pioneering, and driving to possibly demanding.

Defining the I-Scale = Influence

So let's take a look at this picture below. If an 85-100 percent on the I-scale came into this room, how would she naturally respond? What would she do?

HOW YOU PERSONALLY
INFLUENCE PEOPLE AND HANDLE IDEAS

Right! Their response would be excited! "Woohoo! Party! These are all friends I haven't met yet." She would work the room and try to touch 'em all! She would be energized by this experience and talk to as many as he could.

On the other hand, if a 5-10 percent on the I-scale came into this room, how would she respond, especially if she didn't know anyone? Initially, she would rather go home and not even go in. If she had to be there, she would sit in the first empty seat she finds in the back by the door. Eventually, if someone initiated a conversation she would talk to the one or two at the table and hardly move all night, except for food or to go to the restroom. Then she would come right back to her table again. A room like that is totally out of her comfort zone. Those on the left side of the I-scale prefer small groups and deeper conversations with one or two people.

When it comes to ideas, your 50-100 percent I-Parrots (right side of the I-scale) tend to be brainstormers. They have lots of great ideas and tend to fly at 60,000 feet. Remember a lot of the time they are just processing outside their bodies or "ideating." Whereas your 0 percent-50 percent Is (left side of the I-scale) are your "anchors to reality or the tether to the balloon." If the two opposites on the scale are working together, the anchor to reality is usually saying, "Um, I hate to rain on your parade or burst your bubble about your great idea, but really what does that look like and how are we going to do that? Because I am on the ground, you're flying at 60,000 feet. And the reality is, I'm probably the one who is going to be doing the work to make this happen and you're not."

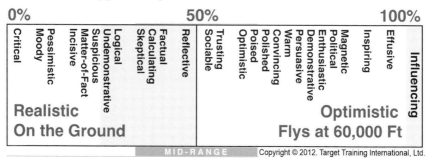

So as you can see, the natural response of those who score 0-50 percent on the left side of the I-scale, when it comes to ideas and people they tend be more: reflective, factual, calculating, logical, matter of fact, undemonstrative, and incisive to the point of being critical.

While those who score 50-100 percent on the I-scale on the right side of the I-scale tend to be more: sociable, trusting, optimistic, poised, convincing, warm, persuasive, magnetic, inspiring, demonstrative, enthusiastic, verbal processor, and full of ideas. Again, neither is right or wrong, nor is one better than the other. We're just different. Both are needed.

DEFINING THE S-SCALE = STEADINESS

The third category of the DISC we need to look at is the S column or steadiness factor. Let's start by taking a look at the pictures below. What do you see in these pictures below?

THE S-SCALE IS HOW YOU PERSONALLY HANDLE PACE AND CHANGE

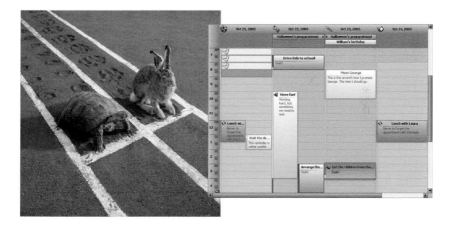

In the picture on the left, you see two polar opposite responses—the hare which is fast, spontaneous, dynamic, impulsive, and the tortoise, which is slow, steady, consistent, and predictable. Also, you can see a schedule with lots of white space. The right side of the S-scale thrives on planning, routines, and having a relaxed, balanced schedule while the left side of the scale feels suffocated by routines, schedules, and plans. They prefer to take a spontaneous "cross that bridge when they come to it," free and flexible kind of approach.

Let's look at this in the context of taking a vacation. What would each side of the scale's vacation look like? The right side of the S-scale, the 50-100 percent would prefer a relaxed pace, with downtime between activities. They would know exactly where they are going, where they are staying, and would have an itinerary of the week's plans. They may even have their annual trips, because they like to know where they are going and what to expect and are not in favor of going where they haven't been before. "Sure things" are a good thing for the S-Doves.

Whereas, the left side of the S-scale, the 0 percent-50 percent might have a plane ticket, but they prefer to "fly by the seat of their pants"—wake up and see where the adventure takes us today; we'll figure it out as we go and see what we feel like at the moment. They prefer to have no routines, like to keep things flexible, free, spontaneous, and variety-oriented while moving a fast pace.

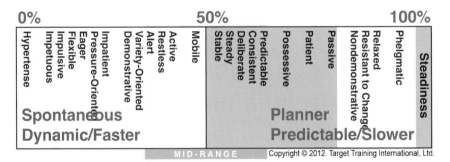

So, as you can see, in the context of pace and change, the 0-50 percent on the left side of the S-scale tend to be: mobile, active, restless, variety-oriented, fast, demonstrative, impatient, eager, flexible, and impulsive. These are your dynamic, spontaneous, go-with-the-flow kind of people who thrive best when things are free and flexible, even unpredictable. On the other side of the S-scale, the 50-100 percent S-Doves tend to be: steady, deliberate, consistent, predictable, possessive, patient, passive, nondemonstrative, resistant to change, relaxed.

Now wait a minute—the words possessive and resistant to change don't seem to fit in that S-Dove list. Let me give you an example. Let's imagine a 90 percent S-Dove—the week is before her and in her head, it is all mapped out as to what she will be doing, where, and when. All of a sudden, her D-Eagle friend, spouse, or boss flies into her life saying, "We're changing things up. I know we made other plans, but scrap that! We're changing gears and we're going over here now. Come on, hurry up! Let's go!"

I always ask my S-Doves to be honest and tell me how that makes them feel. I ask them, "Would it be fair to say in that context, you might become a little possessive of your plan and resistant to change?" The answer is always a resounding, "Yes!" If you are going to do that to an S, you had better have a really good reason. Otherwise, your S-Dove will still be sweet to you, but she will be digging in her heels and still going in the same direction she was planning to go. In some cases, the S-Dove may accommodate, but in a very passive-aggressive way. This is similar to the child at the dinner table where the parents are saying, "Sit down and eat your food!" And the child responds, "I may be sitting down on the outside, but I am standing up on the inside!"

The bottom line is: Don't do that to the S-Doves in your world. Give them plenty of advance notice, time to respond, time to adjust to the change, then it will go well with you. If there is feedback, information, or a decision that needs to be made, don't expect them to give you an answer today. Maybe tomorrow. You can ask them, "When could I expect an answer from you?" Give them time to check their schedule and then respond. Remember, you need each other and your S-Doves are the glue that holds things together. If you keep changing things on them or rushing them, you will break trust and not be the security they need, and they will fly away to find a safer place to be.

DEFINING THE C-SCALE = COMPLIANCE

The C is really measuring the Compliance factor. So in these pictures below you can see there are two polar opposites as well, the rule followers and the risk-takers and rule-breakers.

HOW YOU PERSONALLY HANDLE
RULES AND PROCEDURES SET BY OTHERS

A great way to explain this is to put yourself in the following scenario and see how you naturally respond. I demonstrate this by asking for two volunteers, a 5 percent C and a 95 percent C, so everyone can observe the two completely different responses to the exact same scenario presented.

Example: Imagine that I am approaching you and in a firm way telling you, "I need you to do A, B, and C—IN THE ORDER of 1, 2, and 3! What would be your natural response? Be totally honest.

As you would easily see, those on the 0-50 percent side of the C-scale immediately bristle. They usually ask, "Why do I need to do it that way?" I received this response because I just imposed something on them and confined them to a set of rules which were made for breaking in their book. They were born to challenge the status quo, to color outside the lines, to come up with many different ways of doing things, be free, innovative, pioneering, and not do things in the exact order requested. They will get it done, but not in that order, and they may come up with a new and even better way of doing things.

Then on the other side of the scale, your 50-100 percent C-Owls are so happy to have clear instructions. The clearer the better. They are taking notes and ready to jump in to do it exactly in that order following it to the letter. They may even ask a few more questions and check in to make sure they are doing what is expected, in the way expected, in the time frame required, because they want to do it really well. Remember, one is not better than the other, nor is either good or bad. Both are needed, though one can easily annoy the other. But now with this new understanding, instead of being annoyed we can celebrate our differences, because we are different!

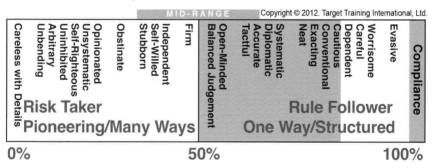

MID-RANGE   Copyright © 2012. Target Training International, Ltd.

| Careless with Details | Unbending | Arbitrary | Uninhibited | Self-Righteous | Unsystematic | Opinionated | | Obstinate | | Stubborn | Self-Willed | Independent | | Firm | | Balanced Judgement | Open-Minded | | Tactful | Accurate | Diplomatic | Systematic | | Neat | Exacting | Conventional | Cautious | | Dependent | Careful | Worrisome | | Evasive | | Compliance |

Risk Taker
Pioneering/Many Ways

Rule Follower
One Way/Structured

0%   50%   100%

So now with that context in mind, when you put things on a 0 percent-50 percent C, you will see this kind of response: firm, independent, stubborn, opinionated, unsystematic, abitrary, unbending, to the point of even careless with the details. So my advice to you is when doing life with a 0-50 percent non-compliant C don't put things on them or micromanage them. Just don't do it! You will trigger those kinds of responses every time and it won't be what's best for you or them. So what should you do instead? Give them the goal of what needs to be accomplished and the deadline, then turn them loose and let them get it done their way. Choices are a beautiful thing for our non-compliant 0-50 percent Cs.

It is a valuable exercise to take your *Descriptors* pages (found near p.10 in your assessment) and put them next to each other. This allows you to visually see where you, your spouse, family, friends, and co-workers respond differently. This also helps you to understand each other better, know what you need, can begin to extend grace, and meet the needs of others as well.

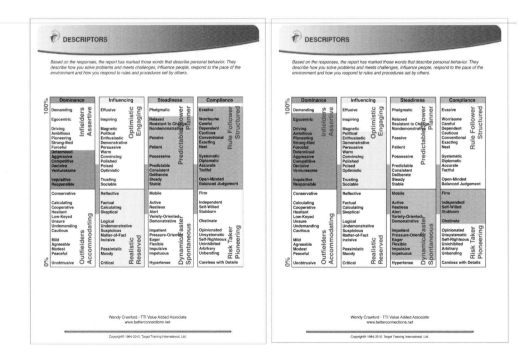

CHAPTER 6

BLENDING DISC BEHAVIOR STYLES

It is futile to put personality ahead of character,
to try to improve relationships with others
before improving ourselves.
~ Stephen Covey ~

*N*ow that you have learned about each of the different behavior styles, you can look at your assessment and see which styles are most prominent for you. Take a look at your Insights® Graph located near page 20. Look at the Natural Graph on the right-hand side of the page to see which ones are most prominent. You may have one, two, or even three of the bars coming up above the 50 percent midline or what TTI calls the "Energy Line."

In this section, I will give you examples of how the various behavior styles play out in your life, blend together, and what you may observe in others as well. You will find yourself and others actually going in and out of these different behavior styles or "modes" and some of them are actually in conflict with each other. I always joke about how all of us are slightly schizophrenic. This combination and blending of styles makes you even more unique. Through TTI's research and development, they have determined there are over 20,000 possible graph combinations, then for the online assessments they pared it down to 384 of the most common graphs. Of all the DISC assessments available on the market, TTI is the only one that has extensively researched and validated their assessments to be about 90 percent accurate.

I truly believe that whenever there is a breakdown in any relationship it is due to either a misunderstanding or being misunderstood. As I walk through the blending of behavior styles, think of how these play out in your life and how you have seen them play out in others as well.

THE DI OR ID (DOMINANCE/INFLUENCE): Both the ID/DI process everything outside the body at a fast rate. They have a sense of urgency and are usually ten steps ahead of the CS/SCs in pace and thought. With this blending, the I actually softens the D. So the D comes across still direct, yet in a nicer, friendlier way. For you personally, there are times you may find yourself in D-mode, making decisions, solving problems, task-oriented, moving fast and furious towards your destination, but then you encounter people and the ideas start flowing which can throw off your forward D momentum. Commonly when you encounter other IDs, they can be cruising along through life in I-mode and at various times the D strikes in its direct, non-candy-coated kind of way, then switches right back to I-mode.

Most of the time the ID/DI isn't even aware they did this, but everyone else is. From their I-mode again they respond, "What? What's wrong? Why are you upset?" If you are an ID/DI, has this ever happened to you where others around you were upset, but you were unaware as to why? Your D probably struck them and you didn't realize it. So it is beneficial to let people know how their behaviors are affecting you in your relationships. It is always good to clarify, "What did you mean by that?" Because many times, that's not the D's intent at all, it just came out that way in their strong demeanor and tone of voice. Remember that's just their unfiltered D coming at you. Once you understand the D's strike, it will help you not to take it as personally, because of the new understanding you have of the DISC Behavior styles. Freedom!

THE SC OR CS (STEADINESS/COMPLIANCE): In this blended style, the two are complementary to each other. Both of the blended styles process at a slower rate, need time to think and respond, process everything inside their bodies, and like to plan and analyze. The CS/SC does not like to take risks. The S-mode likes to schedule and plan, leaving plenty of downtime in between projects or activities. Neither mode wants to be rushed. The C-mode is the part that is detail-oriented and analytical. When a CS/SC creates a schedule along with the plan, it will be followed to the letter in concrete sequential order making sure all the proper steps are taken. If you ever have a disagreement with a SC/CS, you can expect him to build his case and come back the next day or two to present his well-thought-out, logical case. If forced to change directions without reason or logical facts, expect some stubbornness or passive/aggressive behavior to demonstrate itself. I love what Danny Silk says, "If you ever get in an argument with a C, just be quiet, because you're probably wrong!"

Each of the following blended behavior styles are what TTI calls a "Me/Me Conflict," which means for these combination of styles there is an inner struggle that occurs because the two styles are actually in conflict with each other.

THE DC OR CD (DOMINANCE/COMPLIANCE): Both the D and C modes are extremely task-oriented, like to stick to business, and don't leave much time for socializing unless there is a purpose for it. The D part has a high need to be fast and driven, where the C part wants to pull back on the reins to slow things down to analyze or perfect things, causing great inner conflict. One part is fast, the other slow. One part is big picture, the other is concerned with the details. The interesting thing about the DC/CDs is they have the vision and also know exactly how to get there. Their C part will have taken their vision and created a detailed plan in which they'll delegate and expect others to follow it precisely as instructed. Both the D and C parts may have a hard time relinquishing the control, and you can be sure that they will be checking in to see that things are progressing according to plan.

THE DS OR SD (DOMINANCE/STEADINESS): Once again conflict arises because the D mode is quick in decision making, has a sense of urgency, is results-oriented and direct. Once out of the D mode, the S mode has to kick in to bring back the harmony and peace that was disrupted by the directness of the D mode. As a DS, I love what Jackie Durant, Director of Hope City says, "Oh bummer, I need to go back into pastoral mode to clean up the mess my D just made." The D mode has the vision, the S mode has the timeframe. As a DS/SD, you may set goals to achieve your vision, but both modes lack the detail and logical steps on how to actually turn your vision into a reality. You as a DS/SD are at your best when you have a trusted close-knit team that you can direct to see your vision achieve results in a desired timeframe. The DS/SD never gives up because the D part will always take risks and be restless for change which inturn causes your S to step outside of its comfort zone.

THE IS OR SI (INFLUENCE/STEADINESS): When in I-mode, the I is fast, random, ideates, loves people, yet can switch to S mode at other times when they slow everything down. What's interesting about this blended style is that they can have what I like to call a "warm-up factor." If they are in a room full of strangers, you may never see their I mode come out. Once they get comfortable, feel safe, and have begun to get to know those around them, then their I may emerge, but it usually takes a while. Another aspect that most IS or SI blends will admit is that they have lots of "to-dos or good intentions." They may have even scheduled what those look like on the calendar. Yet, as soon as the I-mode kicks in or they encounter people, they can get easily distracted and their whole plan could go out the window thus having good intentions that don't always happen as originally planned because they were distracted by all the people they were interacting with.

THE IC OR CI (INFLUENCE/COMPLIANCE): Many times the IC/CI can feel overwhelmed when their I factor throws them off. What I mean by this is that in I mode they are so fully present with people in the moment that they forget what time it is. Yet the C part hates being late. They end up rushing off to their next destination so they won't be late, but their C is consciously aware that they were speeding the whole way. The C factor needs permission and doesn't like to break the rules. After being in I mode, when they switch over to C mode, they realize they don't have enough time to get everything done as perfectly and accurately as they wanted to. Aaahhhhh! The C part of them wants everything organized, neat, accurate, and thorough. All the while, the I factor comes in and messes it all up again.

Now you further understand how our behavior styles can feel slightly schizophrenic as we go in and out of these various modes. Isn't it good to know you are not crazy! It just feels like it sometimes when you switch back and forth or are doing life with others who are so different from you. It is my prayer that you would have a deeper revelation and understanding into each of these behavior styles and their blending. I love this quote by Stephen Covey, "We see the world not as it is, but as we see it."[2] It is my hope with all you are learning, you will begin to see yourself and others through the new lenses of the DISC and Motivators language.

CHAPTER 7

SPEAKING EACH OTHER'S LANGUAGE

We immediately become more effective
when we decide to change ourselves
rather than asking things to change for us.

~ Stephen Covey ~

*R*emember in the beginning how I mentioned that learning about DISC Behaviors is much like speaking foreign languages? If I continue to speak Spanish and my husband, co-worker, or friend speaks French, does not know any Spanish, and I keep coming at them in Spanish all day long, how well are we going to get along and communicate? Not very well.

If you want to improve your connection and your relationships, a great place to start is by learning each other's DISC Behavior language and what truly motivates the people you do life with. Understanding yourself and others is the first step to enhancing your relationships and developing effective communication. It is so absolutely crucial that we learn how to ADAPT to one another in our relationships. Repeat after me:

It's all about my approach!
I must ADAPT and change my approach to have
better connections, communication and relationships.
And it all starts with me!

Now that you understand the DISC language and you are able to better identify those you do life with, this chapter will give you "Communication Tips" as to how to speak each other's language and approach each other for a win-win encounter. At this point in my workshops, I like to have everyone in the room stand up and gather in the four corners of the room according to their highest percent in the DISC. I use the following *Communications Tips* chart to walk the groups through changing their approach so that they can learn how to adapt and adjust to the other behavior styles.

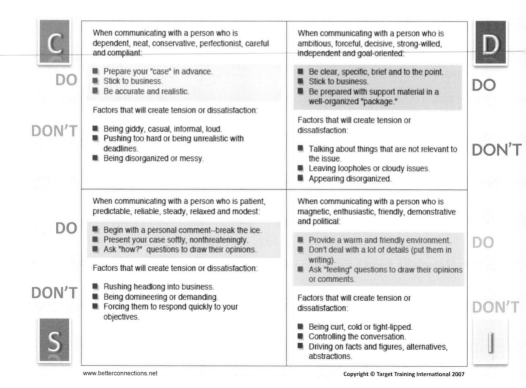

C

DO

DON'T

When communicating with a person who is dependent, neat, conservative, perfectionist, careful and compliant:

- Prepare your "case" in advance.
- Stick to business.
- Be accurate and realistic.

Factors that will create tension or dissatisfaction:

- Being giddy, casual, informal, loud.
- Pushing too hard or being unrealistic with deadlines.
- Being disorganized or messy.

When communicating with a person who is ambitious, forceful, decisive, strong-willed, independent and goal-oriented:

- Be clear, specific, brief and to the point.
- Stick to business.
- Be prepared with support material in a well-organized "package."

Factors that will create tension or dissatisfaction:

- Talking about things that are not relevant to the issue.
- Leaving loopholes or cloudy issues.
- Appearing disorganized.

D

DO

DON'T

DO

DON'T

When communicating with a person who is patient, predictable, reliable, steady, relaxed and modest:

- Begin with a personal comment--break the ice.
- Present your case softly, nonthreateningly.
- Ask "how?" questions to draw their opinions.

Factors that will create tension or dissatisfaction:

- Rushing headlong into business.
- Being domineering or demanding.
- Forcing them to respond quickly to your objectives.

When communicating with a person who is magnetic, enthusiastic, friendly, demonstrative and political:

- Provide a warm and friendly environment.
- Don't deal with a lot of details (put them in writing).
- Ask "feeling" questions to draw their opinions or comments.

Factors that will create tension or dissatisfaction:

- Being curt, cold or tight-lipped.
- Controlling the conversation.
- Driving on facts and figures, alternatives, abstractions.

S

DO

DON'T

I

www.betterconnections.net

Once everyone is gathered in their respective corners, you could already see the DISC dynamics beginning to play out. The D-Eagle and I-Parrots' half of the room is very loud. I usually have a hard time reeling the I-Parrots back in. The hardest part is to get them to stop talking. The other half of the room where the S-Doves and C-Owls is much quieter. The D-Eagles are ready to get this party started. The I-Parrots are laughing and carrying on, the S-Doves are quietly preparing themselves for what this exercise might entail, and the C-Owls are awaiting my instructions and will want to know all the details.

I always start with the D-Eagles first, because they are ready to "get 'er done" plus this gives the S-Doves time to process and know what to expect for when it's their turn. I begin by telling the D-Eagles, "You are going to interact with and approach the S-Doves. Tell me in what ways will you need to adapt your style in order to have a win-win encounter with them? What would you need to do?" On the chart they see they need to: begin with a personal comment or break the ice, present their case softly, non-threateningly, and ask "how" questions to draw out their opinions. Then I ask, "What wouldn't you do?" Many times Ds respond, "Everything that we normally do! We wouldn't force them to respond quickly, rush them, be solely about business, or be domineering and demanding."

Next it is the S-Dove's turn, "Ss you are going to approach the Ds. Tell me in what ways will you need to adapt your style to have a win-win encounter with them? What would you need to do?" Even in this moment, it's appropriate to give the Ss time to think and process. I remind the Ds to notice the processing that is going on before the Ss begin to speak and not to rush them. Then Ss respond, "We'd need to cut to the chase by being direct, specific, and brief, talk faster, stick to business, be prepared, and be organized."

My favorite one-liner to sum it all up is, "Be brief, be bright, be gone." It is then that I like to interject and bring up the topic of writing emails. I like addressing the C-Owls and S-Doves by asking them, "What would your emails look like if you were emailing a D-Eagle?" To their surprise I answer saying, "Subject line is sufficient." Most Ds and Is admit they don't read to the bottom of long emails; they prefer bullet points and will skim the rest. This is painful for the C-Owls to hear. This is the reality we live in with behavior styles in this technology age. In one of the teambuilding sessions I was facilitating, the suggestion was made when we email each other, let's skip the hello part and just write a few bullet points about what you need. The Ss admitted they would have a hard time with that because it felt way too impersonal, while the Cs struggled with having to cut out the details that they felt others really needed to know.

Next, I move onto the C-Owls and the I-Parrots. Again, I'd start with the Is so the Cs can have time to organize their thoughts. In addressing the I-Parrots my instructions are, "If you are going to approach the Cs. Tell me in what ways will you need to adapt your style to have a win-win encounter with them? What would you need to do?" This is where I remind everyone about the "personal space bubble" and that in all actuality most people don't like being hugged, lest you are invited. The Is are hysterical when they do this because its painfully obvious that they're adapting their I down—so much so that it's comical. They try to respond calmly, "We need to try to stick to business, be accurate and realistic, prepare the details in advance, and anticipate the questions they might ask." I always like to ask the Is, "How hard is that for you to do?" The Is expressively say, "Really hard!" Then I ask, "Would you hug them? And Cs, would you like to be hugged?" The answer is usually a resounding, "No!" Then I ask, "What wouldn't you do?" Many times Is respond,

"Be ourselves! We wouldn't talk too much, be loud and casual, be too idealistic and unrealistic with deadlines, random or disorganized." Next it's the Cs turn, "Cs, you are going to approach the Is. Tell me in what ways will you need to adapt your style to have a win-win encounter with them? What would you need to do?" Again this is pretty comical to see the Cs trying to speak the I's language. The Cs respond, "We would provide a warm and friendly environment, ask feeling questions and let them talk, leave the details back at the office, but put the details in writing and send them a brief email recapping what was most important later." Then I ask, "What wouldn't you do?" The Cs respond, "Be all about business, driving on facts and figures, or control the conversation."

This is an enlightening moment, because many of them gained a new self-awareness through this experience of how to better approach people. They are learning what works and what doesn't. They are learning how to honor others and what helps to create positive connections with those who are not like us. Remember, we all can adapt for a while in order to build trust, improve communication, and foster better connections.

A way to help this information sink in so it can produce transformation in your relationships is to take time to observe your friends, family, and co-workers and begin to identify which DISC behavior language you see coming to the surface most often. Then write the names of your friends, family, and co-workers next to the corresponding quadrant on the *Communication Tips* chart. Also, as you read through the following lists write their names next to their respective D, I, S, or C list as well. Study the list and be more intentional about those "Dos and Don'ts" when interacting with your family, friends, and teammates.

When reviewing the following lists, remember to take into consideration each person's blended style and which behavior mode you may need to adapt to given the situation. The following is a more extensive list of the Dos and Don'ts in Communicating for each DISC behavior style:

D-EAGLES DOS AND DON'TS:

- Be clear, specific, and to the point—don't ramble on, or waste their time.
- Stick to business—don't try to build a personal relationship or chitchat.
- Come prepared with all requirements, objectives, and support material in a well-organized package—don't forget or lose things, be unprepared or disorganized.
- Present the facts logically; plan your presentation efficiently—don't leave loopholes.
- Ask specific questions, preferably "What?" questions—don't ask rhetorical questions, or useless ones.
- Provide alternatives and choices for making their decisions—don't come with the decision made or make it for them.
- Provide facts and figures about probability of success or the effectiveness of options—don't speculate wildly or offer guarantees you can't provide.
- If you disagree, take issue with the facts—don't take issue with the D personally.
- Provide a win/win opportunity—don't force the D into a losing situation.
- Keep your distance, use direct eye contact, provide a strong handshake.

I-Parrots Dos and Don'ts:

- Plan interaction that supports their dreams and intentions—don't legislate or muffle.
- Allow time for relating and socializing—don't be curt, cold, or tight-lipped.
- Talk about people and their goals—don't drive to facts, figures, and alternatives.
- Focus on people and action items—put details in writing.
- Don't leave decisions up in the air—ask for their opinion.
- Don't control the conversation—allow them to brainstorm and ideate. After ask, "What did you decide?"
- Don't be impersonal or task-oriented—connect with them on a personal level and listen so they feel heard.
- Use enough time to be stimulating, fun, fast-moving—don't cut the meeting short or be too businesslike.
- Provide testimonials from people they see as important or have influence.
- Don't talk down to them.
- Offer special, immediate, and extra incentives for their willingness to take risks.
- Don't take too much time—get to action items.
- Touch them, hug them, and smile lots.
- Use expressive gestures.
- Do remind them—they welcome reminder texts, emails and voicemails.
- Stand or sit next to them.

S-Doves Dos and Don'ts:

- Start with personal comments. Break the ice—don't rush headlong into business or the agenda.
- Show sincere interest in them as people—don't be only about the business.
- Patiently draw out their personal goals and ideas. Listen and be responsive—don't force a quick response to your objectives or agenda.
- Present your case logically, softly, non-threateningly—don't threaten with positional power or be demanding.
- Ask specific (preferably "How?") questions—don't interrupt as they speak. Listen carefully.
- Move casually, informally—don't be abrupt and rapid.
- If the situation impacts them personally, look for hurt feelings—don't mistake their willingness to go along for satisfaction.
- Provide personal assurances and guarantees—don't promise something you can't deliver.
- If a decision is required of them, allow them time to think—don't force a quick decision or force them to provide information quickly.
- Don't sit too close—lean back, don't rush.
- Be relaxed.
- Use small hand gestures and a calm tone of voice.

C-OWLS DOS AND DON'TS:

- Prepare your case in advance—don't be disorganized, messy, or haphazard.
- Approach them in a straightforward, direct way—don't be casual, informal, or personal.
- Use a thoughtful approach. Build credibility by looking at all sides of each issue—don't force a quick decision.
- Present specifics, and do what you say you will do—don't be vague about expectations or fail to follow through.
- Draw up an "Action Plan" with scheduled dates and milestones—don't overpromise as to results, set reasonable timeframes or goals and be conservative.
- Take your time, but be persistent—don't be abrupt and rapid or rush them.
- If you disagree, prove it with data, facts, or testimonials from respected people—don't appeal to opinions or feelings as evidence or proof.
- Provide them with the information and the time they need to make a decision—use incentives to get a decision.
- Allow them their space—don't touch them.
- Sit or stand across from them.
- Use direct eye contact and little or no hand gestures.

Adapted from *The Universal Language DISC Reference Manual*
Copyright 2011 Target Training International, Ltd

CHAPTER 8

UNDERSTANDING THE INSIGHTS® GRAPHS AND WHEEL

The better you know yourself, the better
your relationship with the rest of the world.

~ Toni Collette ~

The Insights® Graphs and Insights® Wheel provide additional pictures of your preferred environment, natural wiring, and how you may or may not be adapting to your current environment. These visuals give a quick snapshot of you, what you prefer, and gives me as your life coach insight into the areas where you might be adapting significantly. In those areas, I can ask more questions to help identify the sources that could be causing you added stress, fatigue, and dissatisfaction due to an unhealthy adaptation.

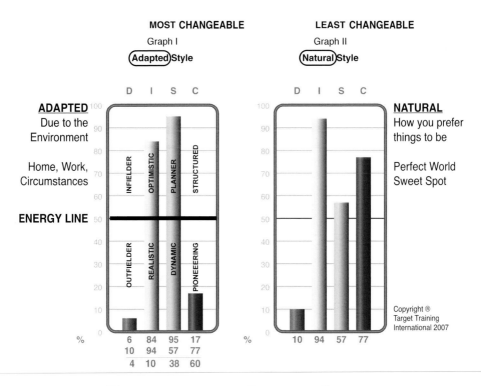

UNDERSTANDING THE INSIGHTS® GRAPHS

The Natural Style graph, located on the right above (found near page 20 in your assessment) tells you what percent you are naturally in the D, I, S, and C, so you can see which side of the scale you are on as discussed in Chapter 5. Your Natural Style is your perfect world, sweet spot, ideal environment, how you prefer things to be. However, the reality is we don't live in a perfect world. We all live in an environment to which we adapt. The graph on the left is your Adapted Style, which is due to your environment, home, work, school, or current circumstances that you may be going through and can be a combination of all of the above.

The first thing I do as a coach is subtract the percentages from each other as shown above. When there is ten points or more disparity in an area, this is where I ask questions in the context of the D, I, S, and C factors. Why? Because the graphs indicate that something is causing you to move away from your preferred "original design" and you are having to be someone you were not created to be. Any time you are adapting ten points or more, you have to exert energy to adapt your behavior style. Studies by Judy Suiter and Dr. David Warburton have shown that exerting that kind of energy over a long period of time can cause stress and fatigue which leads to job dissatisfaction and emotional and physical health issues.[2]

When I see a disparity, I begin my triage analysis to find out more, and zone in on the areas of the disparity. In the example graph shown, I would address this person's S and C. Starting with S, I would ask, "Is there something in your environment that is causing you to have to be more spontaneous, faster paced, flexible? Has an area of your life become more unpredictable, unknown, or not as stable as you would prefer? Possibly the demands on your time have changed and you are not able to finish what you started due to juggling multiple projects?" If the answer is no, then most a Motivator or Strength is being met.

Yet, 90 percent of the time, the answer is an emphatic "Yes!" Then I ask, "Is this causing you stress or fatigue?" If yes, then we explore more and try to identify what the causes could be. Next I ask, "Are there any changes you could make so that you wouldn't have to adapt so much all the time?" If yes, then we explore options that could be implemented to bring things back closer to their original design. If the answer is, "No, I'm trapped!" Then I ask the hard questions, "So, if in one, two, or five years from now, nothing ever changes and things are still exactly the same, are you going to be okay? How long can you continue on if nothing ever changes?" It is then you realize, "Not much longer! I don't care what it costs me. I'll do whatever it takes to make a change!" Why? Because the reality is you're surviving, not thriving. There are specific things you were created for and that you're good at. Remember, God didn't design you to do everything. He designed you specifically to do a number of things really well. Like Graham Cooke says, "In that place is all your permission, favor, and authority."[3]

I had a client who came to me feeling overwhelmed with life. Rightfully so, as one of her children had special needs. As we looked over her assessment, we could see she naturally scored 10 percent on the S-scale, which meant she preferred freedom, flexibility, a fast pace, spontaneity, variety, and not having a set schedule. At the time, she was adapting to a 75 percent S. Why? Because of her situation with her special needs child. Her life had dramatically changed and so had her schedule. She was the one who became the main caregiver, had to quit her job, and took her child to the countless doctor appointments, surgeries, therapies, and activities. She had lost her freedom, flexibility, and ability to be spontaneous, because now she had a schedule that was filled with things that were not her own. When I asked her my triage of questions, she responded, "Yes, I'm feeling it. I'm stressed. I'm surviving and I'm stuck." When I asked her the hard questions, she saw the reality of her adapting and realized she couldn't continue on the way things were for much longer. Because we were able to identify where she was adapting the most through her assessments, she was then motivated to explore her options versus staying stuck. When I asked her, "Are you the one who has to do everything all the time?" For the first time in her life, she realized she didn't have to be the one to do it all. Her newly discovered insights changed her perspective on things and gave her permission to begin exploring new options. This led her to getting the help she needed, so she could get a piece of her life back and not have to adapt so much.

I want you to think of the people in your life who are energized. Why do they have such a zeal for life? These are the ones who have made adjustments to their environments, so they are doing more of what they love, which energizes them on a daily basis because they are in their "sweet spot." DISC is not the only indicator to lead you to your "sweet spot." DISC is how you do what you do and respond to your environment. It is also a tool to help you create your ideal environment and improve your relationships along with your understanding of others. As you learned previously, Motivators are key indicators in helping you to identify what truly fulfills you and satisfies you, which is essential. I always recommend that you don't just look at DISC. I always bring in as much as I can: motivators, strengths, passion, soft skills, talents, hard skills, love languages, core values, spiritual gifts, etc. You could have an environment that matches you perfectly but still not be happy if you're not able to do what truly motivates you and gives you fulfillment and satisfaction.

ADAPTING SCENARIOS:

In review, the context of the D factor is how you handle problems, challenges, and big decisions coming at you. So if you're adapting in any of the D, I, S, or C scales, usually something in your environment has changed to cause you to adapt to that change.

If you're adapting up in your D or more towards the Infielder side of the scale, are you having to be more decisive, assertive, venturesome, competitive, determined? Are you having to make more decisions, handle more challenges or problems than you would prefer? Where are you adapting most: at home, work, school, or due to a current circumstance? If you're adapting down in your D or towards the Outfielder side of the scale, are you having to be more conservative, calculating, cooperative, or agreeable? Are you not being provided opportunities to give your input or be a part of the decision-making process? Are you in a position where your hands are tied and you don't get to direct and decide as much as you would prefer? Do you live with or do life with other strong Ds in which you're adapting your D down and letting them take the lead or make most of the decisions?

In context of the I factor, this is how you influence people and handle ideas. If you are adapting up in your I or moving towards the Optimistic side of the scale, are you having to interact with more people than you would prefer? Do you have to be more social than you prefer? Are you not getting the alone or one-on-one time that you prefer? If you are adapting down in your I or moving toward the Realistic side of the scale, what has changed in your environment? Are you not getting to interact with as many people as you would prefer? Are you in an environment where it's not feasible to share your thoughts and feelings and process your ideas out loud?

Some great examples of this are: you would never take a 5 percent I and make her attend social networking events and trade shows or be continuously presenting and interacting with lots of people. You also wouldn't put her at a receptionist's desk interacting with the public and answering phones constantly. She wouldn't last long. On the other hand, you wouldn't take a 100 percent I-Parrot and put him in a room, close the door, and have him do detailed, routine driven work with no people contact. He would shrivel up and die, because that's just not a good fit for who he is and what he prefers.

In the context of the S factor, this is how you handle pace and change. If your S is adapting up or moving towards the Planner side of the scale, are you having to be more planned, predictable, stable, and steady than you would prefer? Are you having to be more routine driven and scheduled, leaving no room for spontaneity than you would prefer, so much so that it feels somewhat suffocating? If you're adapting down in your S or moving towards the Dynamic side of the scale, is your environment more unpredictable, unknown, and unplanned than you would prefer? Are you having to fly by the seat of your pants, be more spontaneous, and go with the flow more than you would prefer?

In the context of the C, this is how you handle rules and procedures set by someone else. If you are adapting up in your C or moving towards the Structured side of the scale, are you having to be more accurate, systematic, neat, organized, detailed, or compliant than you would prefer? Are there rules and procedures you're required to follow? If you are adapting down in your C or moving towards the Pioneering side of the scale, do you have enough time to finish things with the quality and excellence that you'd like to? Do you have clear expectations and instructions around what you are to be doing? Do you have enough time to analyze, research, and respond, or has something changed?

There was a time in my life when I was adapting from my natural 95 percent C to a 5 percent C. Did I feel it? Absolutely! Was that causing me stress? Yes! I was in a very fast-paced environment where I didn't know what the rules were. There were no rules. There were no instructions. I was on my own to figure it out. I didn't know what I was supposed to be doing because there was no target to aim for. If one was established it moved quickly. As a naturally high-compliant rule follower I was told, "Just go ahead, do it, and ask for forgiveness later." That's a killer for a high compliant C who wants to do everything really well. This forced me to be more independent, unsystematic, arbitrary and careless with details. because I literally did not have the time to be as detailed as I wanted to be. In addition, motherhood and having teenagers increased this reality as well! The good news is through it all, I have learned how to let go of some things.

UNDERSTANDING THE INSIGHTS® WHEEL

The Insights® Wheel adds a visual representation that allows you to:

- View your natural behavioral style (circle)
- View your adapted behavioral style (star)
- Note the degree at which you are adapting your behavior

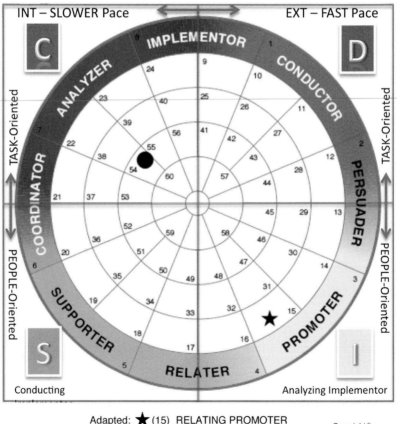

Adapted: ★ (15) RELATING PROMOTER
Natural: ● (54) COORDINATING ANALYZER

The Insights® Wheel provides another picture of the degree of your adapting. The further your dot is from your star, the more you are adapting your behavior. Below are two graphs which show someone in their "sweet spot" and another who is adapting.

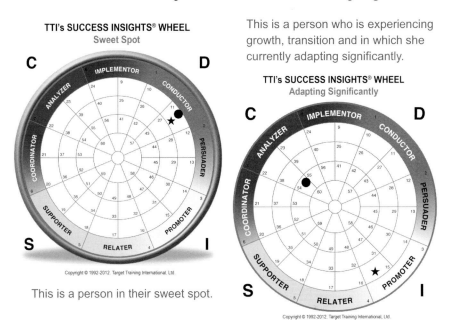

This is a person who is experiencing growth, transition and in which she currently adapting significantly.

This is a person in their sweet spot.

The Wheel also gives us a snapshot of a few others things. As you can see, those whose circle plots on the top half of the wheel (Cs and Ds) tend to be more task-oriented and gain great satisfaction in completing their lists. And yes, even meeting with or talking to a person is considered a task. Sometimes when you walk into a C or D's office you may feel like you're interrupting him, because you are. He is focused and wants to finish what he has started. Those whose circle plots on the bottom half of the wheel (the Ss and Is) are people-oriented and for them it's all about the people. People will always come first over any task that needs to be done in the mind of the I and S.

UNDERSTANDING Me ~ UNDERSTANDING You

As we discussed before, your Cs and Ss prefer a slower pace and process information internally at a slower rate than that of Is and Ds. Your Ds and Is like everything fast, do everything fast, and process everything externally outside their bodies for the whole world to see and hear. The closer your circle is to the center of the wheel shows that it's very easy for you to adapt to the other behavior styles, to the extent that TTI calls this, "The Chameleon." The closer to the outer edge of the wheel shows it is more difficult or uncomfortable for you to adapt to the other behavior styles, especially those on the opposite side of the wheel from you. Everyone can adapt and will benefit by adapting to the other behavior styles when communicating, but it's more uncomfortable for those pure 100 percent D, I, S, and Cs.

Similar to the *Communications Tips* Chart, the Insights® Wheel shows you who your polar opposites are:

- The D's polar opposite is the S, and vice versa
- The I's polar opposite is the C
- The ID's polar opposite is the CS
- The SC's polar opposite is the DI
- The DC's polar opposite is the IS

The high Theoreticals usually ask me about the numbers on the wheel that are from 1-60. The short answer is those numbers mean nothing pertaining to your behavior style. The long answer is, TTI did extensive research to identify the sixty most common graphs and plotted them on the Insights® Wheel which made it very complex. To simplify it, they removed the graphs and assigned a number to each one.

You also may notice the Insights® Wheel is also divided into eight pie shapes. The following are further descriptions of each:

- CONDUCTOR – Getting Results
- PERSUADER – Getting Results Through People
- PROMOTER – Promoting Ideas
- RELATER – Promoting & Implementing Ideas
- SUPPORTER – Implementing the Plan
- COORDINATOR – Implementing & Fine Tuning the Plan
- ANALYZER – Connecting the Plan
- IMPLEMENTER – Thinking & Implementing Creative Ideas

The Insights® Wheel allows you to quickly see where conflict can occur, especially with family members or your teammates. Hopefully, through all that you are learning with the DISC language and Motivators, you have a better understanding of those who are different from you and a new found value for why you need them in your life or on your team.

CHAPTER 9

BRINGING DISC HOME

You don't choose your family.
They are God's gift to you, as you are to them.
~ Desmond Tutu ~

*I*mproving communication and your relationships starts with understanding yourself and others—how you're wired, how you approach life, and how others approach life as well. It is so important to learn how to interact and communicate with each other differently, because we are different. Hopefully, you are beginning to understand the power of DISC in learning about yourself and those you do life with, but don't leave DISC there. Bring DISC home in relation to your spouse, kids, and friends, and utilize this powerful language to enhance all your relationships.

DISC is the language of "people watching." Please keep in mind as you learn about the different DISC behavior styles, this is not meant to put people in a box or label them. It is really meant to help you communicate and understand each other better so that you can honor and celebrate each other even more. So now that you have learned the language, you will have a greater awareness of how these DISC behavior styles play out in your family, marriage, and even with the little ones in the sandbox. In observing the sandbox, here's what you'll see:

- THE D-EAGLES: are the ones who take charge of the sandbox. They're directing and delegating, have big ideas for the sandbox, and are telling the others what to do.

- THE I-PARROTS: are talking to everyone, saying what they see, expressing themselves and their ideas emotionally.and They are having fun while randomly moving from one person to another throughout the sandbox.

- THE S-DOVES: are accommodating and bringing harmony to the sandbox, steadily and faithfully helping others with their projects, and are planning as to when the next play date will be.

- THE C-OWLS: are taking in as much information as they can, paying close attention to details, asking lots of questions, while they are perfecting and finishing what they started with excellence before they move onto the next thing. They're also the rule followers and enforcers of sandbox.

It's so important to understand your children's DISC behavior styles and your spouse's as well, because then you can speak their language and have better heart-to-heart connections. Understanding each other, knowing what you need and they need is vital for thriving healthy family relationships. The following are some more tangible examples of how DISC plays out in our families:

- IF MY SPOUSE is far right on the C-scale and I'm on the opposite side of the scale, it's no wonder he gets frustrated with my resistance to follow status quo and my lack of attention to detail. Now I'm beginning to understand why he doesn't appreciate it when I break the rules and I don't put things back where I got them from. We approach things in totally different ways. What bothers him doesn't bother me. Yet for us to have a better connection, we both need to adapt and meet in the middle.

- IF MY DAUGHTER is far right on the S-scale and I'm on the opposite side of the scale, it's no wonder she becomes anxious every time I change the plans on her, rush her out the door, add additional things to her schedule, or plan things for her. Those are the very things that cause an S to shut down, become anxious, withdraw, or to cause them to dig in their heels. Is it possible that I could change my approach in a way that would reduce some of the anxiety my daughter is experiencing?

- IF MY TEENAGER is far right on the D-scale and I'm on the same side of the scale too, it's no wonder we go toe-to-toe every time I tell him what to do and decide for him. That just doesn't work for a D. Ask any D, they will tell you. Offering him choices is a much better option.

- IF MY FIFTH GRADER is far left on the C-scale or non-compliant, it's no wonder I as his parent have a hard time understanding why he continually challenges the rules, doesn't follow my instructions, and will do things his way in a way I would have never thought of.

- IF MY SISTER is far right on the I-scale, and every time we are together I only stick to the details of what I want to talk about, I show no interest in hearing her latest idea, and don't attend her parties, how well do you think we'll connect? As you can guess, not very well at all. Because I'm not adapting and understanding who she is or appreciating what she likes, our relationship suffers.

To improve your relationships you will need to take what you have learned in DISC, practice adapting, and begin relating to others differently. Learning the language and then changing your approach will be life-changing with your spouse, children, and family members, not just with those on your team or at work. Here are some tips as to how to change your approach and speak your family member's language once you know their DISC behavior style. If your spouse, child, relative, or friend is a:

D – Be clear, specific, brief, and to the point. Bottom line bullet points are sufficient. Stick to business. Be prepared and organized.

I – Provide a warm and friendly environment. Don't deal with a lot of details—write them down. Ask "feeling" questions and let them talk.

S – Begin with a personal comment—break the ice. Present your case softly, nonthreateningly. Ask "How?" questions to draw their opinions.

C – Prepare your case in advance. Stick to business. Be accurate and realistic.

The more you learn about DISC language and implement it into your relationships, the more your relationships, communication, and connections will improve! To access the variety of online assessments go to: www.betterconnections.net or for additional resources go to: DISC-U.org

DISC Can Change Your Family and How You Parent

Through the DISC and Motivators language I learned so much about myself and others. I could not wait for my children to take the assessment so I would know more about them as well. As you can imagine, it was eye-opening. Through the process, God gave me such revelation and a heart for other families to have this insight as well.

As I did more and more family debriefs, I saw a common pattern among families. Usually there is one lone ranger all by himself across the wheel from everyone else or in another quadrant. I thought about how many times someone in the family gets labeled as the "black sheep of the family." The sad reality is that they were simply created to be different and weren't meant to conform to be like the rest of the family. Yet,

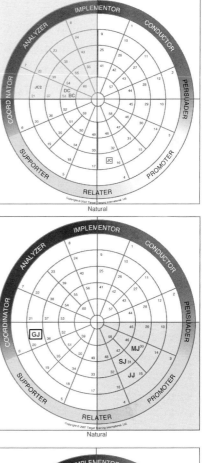

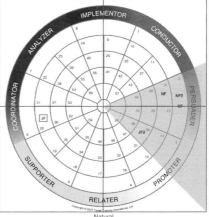

Various Family Wheels with the majority in one quadrant and one family member in another.

time and time again, they were alienated instead of being celebrated for who they were, simply because as a family they didn't know how to celebrate and appreciate someone who is not like the rest of them. If every person took the time to understand and apply the DISC language combined with Danny Silk's, *Culture of Honor* and *Loving our Kids on Purpose*, I believe we would all parent differently. As a result, families and generations would be healthier and have a greater impact in the kingdom of God.

This dynamic has played itself out in my own family with my own children. I remember the Lord speaking to me about one of my kids to stop making him conform to the rest of the family. He showed me the picture of a square peg and a round hole, saying, "Your son is the square peg and you are continually trying to cram him into the round hole of the Crawford family. He is not like the rest of you and has no desire to be. Don't force him to be someone he is not."

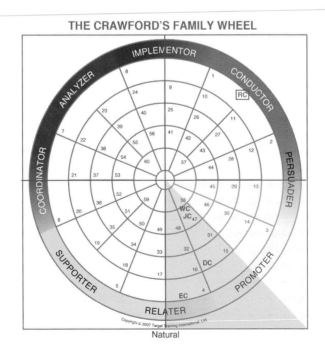

THE CRAWFORD'S FAMILY WHEEL

Natural

I remember just weeping because that's exactly what we were doing and things were not going well for us. No wonder he continually wanted to escape the environment we were creating. I am thankful for the wisdom and revelation of the Lord and for the DISC language that made this so clear to us.

Through the DISC language and Danny Silk's *Loving Our Kids on Purpose*, I learned how to completely change my approach on how I parented my oldest son, my square peg, who did not want to be crammed into that round hole day after day. I learned that he needed choices. It didn't work for me to bark out commands, tell him what he needed to be doing, and then come along behind him to make him meet my standards because his didn't. Because I didn't think he heard me, I learned that repeating myself was actually ruining our connection. Being strict and imposing my values upon him only drove him further away.

The good news is everything I have learned has truly saved our relationship! Because of my understanding of a 100 percent D, instead now I ask him, "When would be a good time to chat?" So he can decide his own timetable. I am trying to remember not to put things on him or to micromanage him. When he says, "Mom, I got this." I have to let go and simply trust him to make good decisions. If he doesn't, then I need to let the consequences of his poor choice be his master teacher, while I "keep my love on." This keeps our connection strong as he learns about real life. Thank you, Danny Silk![2] Now I include my son in the decision-making process and let him come up with his options and then let him decide. We do engage in debates over the limits then come to a reasonable agreement to which he holds himself accountable. He is fully aware of what will happen if he chooses to cross the line due to a poor choice.

Because we are opposite in many ways, we have been learning how to speak each other's DISC behavior language. When I pick him up after practice, the IC part of me wants to hear every detail about his day, his life, and the emotions he's experiencing. He, on the other hand, isn't into details and certainly does not experience emotions the way I do. So our compromise is when he gets in the car, he has agreed to share five detailed bullets points with me about his day, as long as I promise not to ask any more questions or seek more information. Although he would prefer to give me three bullet points and I would prefer a lot more than that, we have agreed on five. This is an example of my behavior style adapting to his and his adapting to mine, which has been critical for our heart-to-heart connection with my 100 percent D teenager.

Then I have my almost 100 percent IS daughter, whom I have learned not to rush. When I rush her, it never goes well for us. I now give her what she needs—the one-hour warning if we need to be somewhere. For her, repetition is really good and absolutely needed because with her 100 percent I, she will forget. With her, I have to be okay with repeating myself, yet remember to not repeat with my D teenager. I also have learned how to coach her when it comes to details as she loves to overcommit herself without considering everything that needs to happen for her to keep the commitments she has made.

My other son, an IC, is very much like me. He is a rule-follower, is compliant and aims to please. Our interactions are easier because we both speak the same language and want the same things. On the following page is a fun example from his childhood along with a couple other examples:

YOU KNOW YOU HAVE A HIGH:

- C CHILD WHEN he gets out of the pool, walks over to the "Pool Rules," reads each and every rule, then turns around and tells everyone what they should and should not be doing! Crack me up! My husband and I laughed and laughed!

- I CHILD WHEN she plans a sleepover with all her friends, but forgets to check the calendar to see that she has two other commitments that night and one the next morning.

- D CHILD WHEN you plan a birthday party that includes some of his favorite things, and he doesn't want to do any of it because it wasn't his idea and because you didn't ask him first.

- S CHILD WHEN you have to wait for her to finish what she started before you can leave and most likely you will be late.

Through observing your children you can learn so much and realize which of your approaches are working and which aren't. Applying what you learned from the *Communication Tips* chart and changing your approach will help you to have better connections with your kids. Learning to speak their DISC behavior language and loving them in their *Love Languages* (by Gary Chapman) are absolutely critical and will make a difference in your relationships.

Through my own self-discovery process of the DISC language, I became keenly aware of my high C and how task-oriented I was. This unfortunately had a direct effect on my children and from the way I had parented them previously. I'm so thankful for the SOZO ministry, as I know each of my children will need a session to gain freedom from the messages that I unintentionally sent their way. SOZO is the Greek word translated "saved, healed, delivered." The Sozo ministry is a unique inner healing and deliverance ministry aimed to get to the root of things that are hindering your personal connection with the Father, Son and Holy Spirit. With a healed connection, you can walk in the destiny to which you have been called.

A Sozo session is a time for the Sozo team to sit down with you and with the help of the Holy Spirit walk you through the process of freedom and wholeness. Sozo is not a counseling session but a time of interacting with Father, Son and Holy Spirit for wholeness and pursuing of your destiny.[3]

So let me explain further how my high C had a direct effect on my children. I was blessed to be able to work from home for the majority of my children's upbringing. Though I was present in body, many times they would come into my office just wanting my attention and affection. But for me, I felt like I couldn't give them my full attention until I completed the task before me, only then could I be fully present for them. Please hear me—there is a delicate balance between teaching your children to wait for a moment and responding to their needs. That is why I'm so thankful for the Holy Spirit and my husband who was able to help me with this. For me, I realized because of my task-orientedness I was beginning to send the message, "Everything that I am doing is more important than you are." My heart broke when I realized that is not the message I wanted to send to my kids. Honestly, this was a struggle for me. I hated being interrupted. I compulsively had to finish what I started. I needed help and I needed God to set me free and help me to let go. I asked my husband to hold me accountable and to ask me at the appropriate times, "Honey, what is really more important right now?" That question put things into proper perspective for me and helped me to let go so I could be the mom my kids needed me to be in that moment, even though my behavior style wanted to pull me in the opposite direction.

As you are becoming fully aware, it is so important to know how your behavior styles and values are affecting your relationships. We must learn how to establish a culture of honor in our homes as well. In his book *Culture of Honor*, Danny Silk defines honor as, "Accurately acknowledging who people are." Honor creates life-giving and life-promoting relationships. Honor is the relational tool that protects the value that people have for those who are different than they are. We can only do this when we learn to recognize other's God-given identities and roles. As a result, a culture of honor can be created as a community of people are able to be themselves in their home environment and in community together.[4]

One of the other vital core values Danny Silk teaches in *Loving our Kids on Purpose* is creating a safe place where people can be free. Free people cannot live together without honor, cannot exist without free people. Honor can only be used successfully amongst powerful people who have a true sense of their personal responsibility in preserving the freedom around them. As you are probably aware, high levels of freedom can generate conflict, usually because we experience others who are approaching life in a different way. Without a core value of honor, we find that our discomfort around those who choose to live in ways that we would not, leads us to shut down their freedom.

It is typical, for example, when a teenager begins to explore his or her freedom, that his or her parents become afraid. The fear stems from the fact that the teenager is choosing options that the parents would not choose for themselves or approve of. The wrestling match escalates as the teenager tries to individuate from his parents and the parents strive to keep the teenager looking like them. The further the teenager moves from how the parents live, the more likely the parents are to step in and shut down the teenager's choices. The result is conflict. But when a teenager and their parents both practice honor, which contains within it love and trust, fear is not allowed to rule their decisions and freedom can be preserved.[5]

CHAPTER 10

DISC CAN CHANGE YOUR MARRIAGE

A great marriage is not
when the 'perfect couple' come together.
It is when an imperfect couple
learns to enjoy their differences.
~ Dave Meurer ~

There is an old saying, "Opposites attract." With DISC you can actually see this when you put your Descriptors pages side by side. Most couples are polar opposites in at least two or three areas of the D, I, S, and C. I will share with you in this chapter some examples of what this means and how it can play out in your marriage in the areas where you are polar opposites.

On the I-scale, if a far left 5 percent I marries a far right 80 percent I, there is going to be some conflict. Why? Because the far right 80 percent I-Parrot spouse loves having parties, wants her spouse to go with her to parties, will have lots of friends, will invite lots of friends over most of the time. She also has lots of ideas, is expressive, talkative, and pretty much will process everything outside her body. Whereas a 5 percent on the far left side spouse is more reflective, prefers one-on-ones and alone time, has a smaller group of a few close friends, doesn't care for parties, or appreciate it when people are invited over at the last minute. He is also realistic, practical, and is considered to be an anchor to reality.

Then there are those who are married and are opposite in the their Ss. The far right on the S-scale, 80 percent S-Dove, prefers a slower, relaxed pace with everything planned out, having a predictable routine, and plenty of downtime. While the far left on the S-scale, 10 percent S, likes a fast pace, variety, change, is spontaneous, does not like doing the same things over and over, has the need to keep things free-flowing and flexible. He actually feels suffocated by schedules and plans. Can you imagine these two going on vacation together? Might there be a need to compromise so they don't drive each other crazy?

Then there are those who are opposite in their C. The far right on the C-scale, 85 percent C-Owl, prefers one way of doing things, focusing on the details, following the rules, structure, keeping things neat, organized, doing things in a specific order, including how to load the dishwasher, clean the house, which way the pans get stacked, right down to which way the toilet paper should be put on. Everything has a place and gets put back in that place. Whereas, the far left, 5 percent C, prefers to not be concerned about the details, to change things up with many different ways of doing things, to be arbitrary, unsystematic, color outside the lines, and likes to challenge status quo. Let's just say the 5 percent C doesn't care much for instructions or like to follow directions, and has the attitude, "Rules, what rules? Rules were made to be broken."

This is where my husband and I are the most opposite. He is a 5 percent C with ADD and I am a 95 percent C. Can you imagine? Have we had conflict? Oh, yes! My favorite story to tell is about our camping experiences. For fifteen years we owned a pop-up tent camper. As you might imagine it was no easy task for my husband to make everything fit into that box because it needed to fold down in a concrete, sequential order. After learning our DISC behavior styles, we switched some of our roles around. I was better wired for packing and folding down the camper and my husband's new role was to pack the car. Honestly, I had to restrain myself to not look in the trunk, because his theory was, "It doesn't matter how it goes in or looks because we are just going to take it out when we get home anyway." These were great lessons in teaching me to simply let go.

After all those years, God blessed us with a different camper. Hallelujah! It's a thirty-foot, pull-behind camper trailer which we absolutely love. Now that we know what we know, I'm the one who hooks up the camper and backs it onto the ten-foot slab next to our garage. Why? Because now it's a safety issue. If it is not hooked up correctly, with that chain this way, these sway bars that way, the brake controller here, this crank turned there, then our safety is at risk along with others. I'm so thankful for all that we've learned about each other through DISC and Motivators. Each has brought me such revelation and freedom! It has freed me from being frustrated. It has given me the insight that my husband just is not detailed, was not made that way, and I need to stop expecting him to be.

On the contrary, if you're alike in some of the areas, there will be conflict as well. The following are some examples:

- If two people marry who are similar on the high D-scale, get ready for some vocal debates of telling each other what they think. It will be important for each one to take turns, so that one isn't adapting all the time.

- If two people marry who are similar on the high I-scale, they will certainly have lots of fun along the way, their biggest fights being over whose social event is more important or whose idea is better.

- If two people marry who are similar on the high S-scale, their biggest conflict will be over their schedules. Your schedule or my schedule, your plan or my plan?

- If two people marry who are similar on the high C-scale, their biggest conflict will be whose way is the right way.

Take a moment to put the *Descriptors* pages of your spouse or your kids side by side (the *Descriptors* page can be found near p.10 in your assessment). Begin to identify the areas in which you are polar opposites. Remember, one is not better than the other, nor is one good or bad. We each are wired to respond to various situations differently. Recall, the eight different sides of DISC, now you have a personalized visual picture of what each person needs and how they respond to handling problems, decisions, crises (D), people and ideas (I), pace of life (S), and rules and procedures set by others (C.) If you want to have peace in your relationships, you will need to be willing to be flexible. Pushing for your own way all the time will only hurt and offend those around you. The good news is no matter how we are wired, we can now begin to understand and value each other in how we are similar and how we are different.

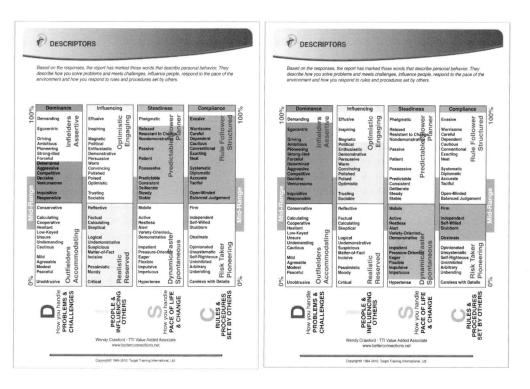

It is important to be aware of what each DISC behavior style needs as well. The following is an enlightening list to keep in front of you when you consider your own needs and the needs of others.

GREATEST NEEDS ARE:

- THE D-EAGLE: Significance, justice, challenge, achievement, and freedom
- THE I-PARROT: Acceptance, to be known, recognition, worth, joy, and fun
- THE S-DOVE: Security, peace, stability, belonging, love, value, and appreciation
- THE C-OWL: Permission, assurance, approval, to do things well, details, and information

IDENTIFYING AND COMMUNICATING NEEDS

The sad reality is that over time what you learned can begin to fade because we all tend to forget. One way to keep DISC alive in your environment is to continue to observe others and speak the language every day. In my workshops I like to ask, "How can you truly honor someone if you don't know what they need?" So many times we think we are honoring someone, when in reality, we have missed the mark because we have not taken the time to really connect with that person and find out what their true needs are. One way of doing that is to get better at communicating to others what you need and being aware of their behavior styles and what motivates them as well. As mentioned before, Motivators are the "why" you do what you do, what fulfills and satisfies you. Once you are aware of the dominant Motivators that are important in your life, you will be able to identify what drives your actions, what fulfills you, and what causes conflict. In addition, understanding and applying Motivators to your relationships with others will deepen your appreciation of them and clarify the "why" of your interactions and others.

The following *His Needs, Her Needs* is an exercise you can walk through with your spouse, family or team. From your assessment and in each area of the D, I, S, C, you will determine what is most important to you. The instructions are as follows:

MOTIVATORS (SEE EXAMPLE ON P.134)

On a piece of paper, create a worksheet similar to what you see on page 135. Next, if you know your top three Motivators write them in the first box (otherwise continue down to the D). For each Motivator, select short sentences or words that best describe what fulfills you and satisfies you most. Now capture only one or two words that best describe what you need and write it in the "REMINDER CODE WORDS" column. Your "CODE WORDS" are your one-liners you will use to communicate to others what you need. On the next page is a sample of a completed worksheet to aid you in completing your own.

D – NEXT TO THE D: write on your side of the worksheet what you need when you have to make big decisions, handle problems, challenges, or crises. Select one word as your "Reminder Code Word" that you can use to communicate to others what you need.

I – NEXT TO THE I: write on your side of the worksheet what amount of people interaction you prefer. Also, write how you prefer to process ideas. Select one or two words as your "Reminder Code Word" that you can use to communicate to others what you need.

S – NEXT TO THE S: write on your side of the worksheet what you prefer when it comes to pace of life and schedule. Also write down what works best for you when there is a change of plans. Select one or two words as your "Reminder Code Word" that you can use to communicate to others what you need.

C – NEXT TO THE C: write on your side of the worksheet what you prefer when it comes to rules and procedures set by someone else. Also write, when it comes to details and information, how much do you prefer? Select one or two words as your "Reminder Code Word" that you can use to communicate to others what you need.

LOVE LANGUAGES –

Write down your top two *Love Languages* and what makes you feel loved. You can take a free assessment to learn more about your *Love Language*s at www.5lovelanguages.com by Gary Chapman.

Then practice, practice, practice utilizing the language everyday everywhere you go. Create a permission-based culture of honor where you are free to tell each other what you need and you know the needs of others as well, so you can truly honor and value one another.

HIS NEEDS 👫 HER NEEDS

MOTIVATORS	REMINDER CODE WORDS		MOTIVATORS
SOCIAL TRAD UTIL To see the purpose, verify costs, don't waste my time, live out faith	Purpose Value	Impact Balance	SOCIAL TRAD INDIVID To help people, make an impact, keep it all in balance, be about my Father's Business
D Handling Decisions, Problems, Challenges My ideas & decisions heard, my list honored Don't tell me, give me choices When I'm frustrated – a soft hand & calm voice	Bullet it Choices Soft touch	TIME Thoughts? More Info	Handling Decisions, Problems, Challenges **D** Time to think & respond Time to research I don't make decisions quickly. Ask for my opinion, but give me time to think & process
I Handling People & Ideas To be listened to Your full attention Social interactions Express my Ideas	Listen to me w/your eyes Ask where did you land?	Obser-vation Me time	Handling People & Ideas **I** To process in DETAIL see & say things out loud Time alone sometimes Quiet time to recharge
S Handling Pace of Life & Change Schedule / Plan / My list To know what to expect Advanced warning Don't RUSH me	Ask, What's the Plan? What's on your list? Calendar?	Make an Appt On my RADAR	Handling Pace of Life & Change **S** Schedule – to know the plan What to expect, Time to plan and time to adjust change directions Advanced notice, time to adjust Not to be rushed
C Rules & Procedures Set by Others Flexibility, freedom, No instructions, Not to be told what to do My own timeframe & My way to do things	Just go with it Ask Permission to Tweak?	TIME Details! Tell me, You need to let go OCD'n	Rules & Procedures Set by Others **C** Information DETAILS!! No chaos No clutter Order Organization Structure To know what's needed Time to process, to do it well Permission
LOVE LANGUAGES Physical Touch Words of Affirmation	Touch & Texts	One-on-one time Do things for me	LOVE LANGUAGES Quality Time Acts of Service

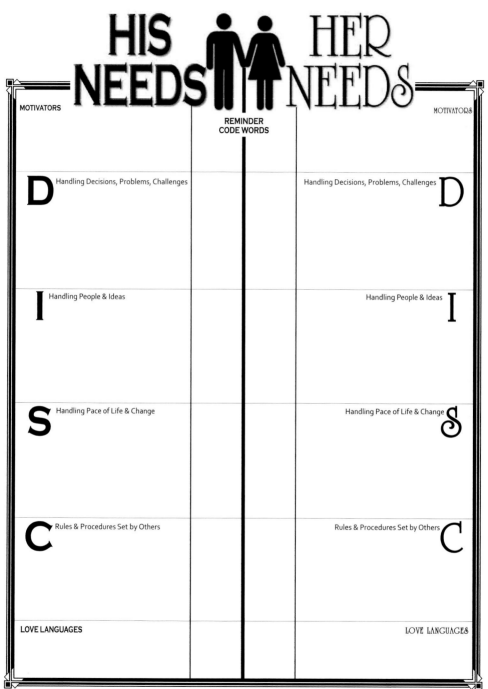

HIS NEEDS HER NEEDS

MOTIVATORS	REMINDER CODE WORDS		MOTIVATORS
D Handling Decisions, Problems, Challenges			Handling Decisions, Problems, Challenges **D**
I Handling People & Ideas			Handling People & Ideas **I**
S Handling Pace of Life & Change			Handling Pace of Life & Change **S**
C Rules & Procedures Set by Others			Rules & Procedures Set by Others **C**
LOVE LANGUAGES			LOVE LANGUAGES

www.betterconnections.net

One of the best examples I have to illustrate this is from my own marriage. Remember, I am a IC and have some S as well. So when I am in my unadapted I-mode, I tend to verbally process everything outside my body in detail (the C part). Lord help me, and those I do life with! Remember the I-Parrot says what they see.

On a typical day in the Crawford home, as one of the kids came through the door, I noticed how squeaky it was and verbalized it by saying, "Man, that door is squeaky." Now in the old days before we knew about the DISC language, that statement would send my husband into "fix-it" mode. With frustration he would respond, "That's one more thing to put on my 'to do' list! I just don't have time to get to it right now!" He responded that way because his D doesn't like to be told what to do and his S already had the day planned out and fixing the door wasn't a part of it. So I responded, "Whoa, time out! I'm not asking you to fix it, that was just an observation." What he didn't understand, I was just processing verbally outside my body what I saw and had no intentions for him to do anything about it. After going through this exercise to identify our needs and learning about our DISC behavior styles, one of our code words is, "Observation." Now when I say, "Wow, that door is really squeaky," He asks, "Observation?" I respond, "Yes, observation!" And now he knows what that observation meant. I didn't need him to fix it, I was just saying what I saw with no intent behind it at all.

CHAPTER 11

DISC CAN TRANSFORM YOUR TEAM

*If people don't feel safe to be themselves
and don't feel a sense of connection with people around them,
then it's hard to convince them that they are in a safe place.[1]*
~ Danny Silk ~

A healthy team is one that recognizes their need for those who are different from them because they bring to the group what is lacking. The perfect team has people of each D, I, S, and C behavior style on the team, at least one in each quadrant on the Insights® Wheel. Typically, there's only one D-Eagle directing the team. Why? Because when you put D-Eagles all together there literally is a pecking order that occurs. One will emerge to the top to direct, command, and delegate, and then the other D-Eagles will fly away. Why? Because they were born to lead, direct, be in charge, command, make decisions, and tell others what to do. The only way it works to have multiple D-Eagles in an organization or on one team is to make sure they each have their own area in which they can lead, direct, have the vision, and be the key decision-maker. If they are not given that opportunity, they will get bored and will find something they can be in charge of because that's what they were born for. "Their fast pace, results-oriented approach is often misunderstood; but with the proper understanding and management, the high D is a tremendous person to have on the team. Not having or wanting a high D on the team puts the team at a great disadvantage,"[2] according to Bill Bonnstetter, President and CEO of (TTI) Target Training International, Ltd.

Next you have your I-Parrots. You need them on your team because they are the ones who grab onto the vision and tell everyone about it. They do the presenting and attend all the networking, trade shows, and social events to tell everyone about the awesome vision, idea, or product, and have a lot of fun while doing so. They also are your brainstormers or your creative expressives who come up with new ideas and are thinking outside the box. They are your event planners, networkers, your "people" people. Without them, things would be boring. They bring the fun to any team.

Then there are your S-Doves. You need lots of these on your team because they are the glue that holds the team and everything together. They accommodate, support, and plan out everything that needs to be done. They also grab onto the vision and actually set things in motion to make the vision or idea happen. Typically it is the S or C that comes alongside to finish what the D or I started and help to turn their vision or idea into a reality. Your S-Doves are happy to work behind the scenes doing the maintenance and routine work that make the Ds and Is look famous. They will do this as long as they know they are valued and appreciated for their contributions to the team.

Last but not least, you have your C-Owls. There are only a few of these on the team as well. They are needed because they take all that was started, determine the next steps, create a structure, organize it, perfect it, and turn it into a well-oiled machine with systems in place so that it can maintain itself. The C-Owls fill in the gaps, cover all the bases, and bring the detail-orientedness that makes something good become excellent.

A perfect team is only perfect when everyone on the team understands and operates in the DISC language, celebrates each other, and is intentional about creating a culture of honor on a daily basis.

Example of a team with the four DISC behavior styles represented

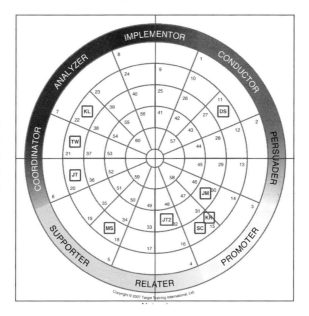

WHAT THE D–EAGLES BRING TO THE TEAM:

- Bottom-line Organizer. Results oriented.
- Self-starter. Given the task, the responsibility, and the authority, Ds will work long hours to get something done.
- Forward Looking. Obstacles represent a challenge that can be overcome.

WHAT THE D–EAGLES BRING TO THE TEAM: *continued*

- Timely. They are always driven for efficiency (quicker, faster, better).
- Challenge-Oriented. If a high D does not have a challenge, he or she will create one.
- Competitive. Are motivated to consistently perform better.
- Initiates Activity. They want to get started and get things done.
- Challenges the status quo. They aren't concerned about the way things have always been done. They are willing to rock the boat to make things better.
- Innovative. They are constantly looking for shortcuts to get things done faster.
- Tenacious. They are driven to results, challenges, and winning.

IDEAL ENVIRONMENT FOR THE HIGH D–EAGLES:

- Freedom from controls, supervision, and details
- Evaluation based on results, not process or method
- An innovative and futuristic oriented environment
- Non-routine work with challenge and opportunity
- A forum for them to express their ideas and viewpoints

POSSIBLE LIMITATIONS OF HIGH D-EAGLES:

- Overstep authority
- Be too directive
- Be impatient with others
- Be argumentative
- Not listen well; be a one-way communicator
- Take on too many tasks
- Push people rather than lead them
- Lack tact and diplomacy
- Focus too heavily on task

VALUE OF THE HIGH I-PARROT TO THE TEAM:

- Optimism and enthusiasm. Great ability to motivate others. They will keep the team together when the going gets tough.
- Creative problem solving.
- Motivaters. Motivates others towards goals through positive interaction and persuasion.
- Positive sense of humor. They add fun to the team and to the task.
- Team Player. They have fun while getting the job done.
- Negotiates conflict. A natural mediator.
- Verbalizes articulately. They will paint an optimistic picture of the possibilities.

IDEAL ENVIRONMENT FOR THE HIGH I-PARROT:

- Assignments with a high degree of people contact
- Tasks involving motivating groups and establishing a network of contacts
- Democratic supervisor with whom they can associate
- Freedom from control and detail
- Freedom of movement
- Multi-changing work tasks

POSSIBLE LIMITATIONS OF HIGH I-PARROTS:

- Oversell
- Act impulsively, heart over mind
- Trust people indiscriminately
- Inattentive to detail
- Have difficulty planning and controlling time
- Overestimate their ability to motivate others or change behavior
- Under-instruct and over-delegate
- Tends to listen only situationally
- Overuse hand motions and facial expressions when talking
- Rely too heavily on verbal ability

VALUE OF THE HIGH S-DOVE TO THE TEAM:

- Dependable team worker. Brings loyalty and stability to the team.
- Supporter. Works hard for a leader and a cause
- Great listener. Natural at helping people work through problems.
- Patient and empathetic. Gives people the benefit of the doubt.
- Good at reconciling. Bring calmness, harmony, and peace.
- Logical and step-wise thinker. Bring lofty ideas back to the realm of reality. Will point out gaps and obstacles.
- Will finish desired tasks. They want to finish a task before moving on to the next. They will develop a system to get the job done.
- Loyal, long-term relationships. They may be able to hold the team together when the going gets tough. They bring strength.

IDEAL ENVIRONMENT FOR THE HIGH S-DOVE:

- Jobs for which standards and methods are established
- Environment where long-standing relationships can be developed
- Personal attention, recognition for tasks completed and well done
- Stable and predictable environment
- Environment that allows time for change
- Small team of people which are willing to be personal, intimate

POSSIBLE LIMITATIONS OF HIGH S-DOVES:

- Take criticism personally
- Resist change just for change's sake
- Need help getting started on new assignments
- Have difficulty establishing priorities
- Internalize feelings when they should be discussed
- Wait for orders before acting
- Give false sense of compliance
- Can be too hard on themselves
- May stay involved in a situation too long
- May not project a sense of urgency

VALUE OF THE HIGH C-OWL TO THE TEAM:

- Objective Thinker. They bring reality to plans.
- Conscientious. They take their work personally and will go the extra mile to get the job done.
- Maintaining high standards. They will help to create the standards.
- Defines, clarifies, gets information, criticizes, and tests. They are great objective thinkers. Their skeptical nature looks at all possibilities before they buy into a plan.
- Task-Oriented. Urgency on doing tasks.
- Asks the right questions. They will ask the tough questions, challenge things for improvement.
- Diplomatic. They are very diplomatic with sharing data. They prefer discussions that are void of a lot of emotion.
- Detail-Oriented. Pays attention to small details.

IDEAL ENVIRONMENT FOR THE HIGH C-OWL:

- Where critical thinking is needed and rewarded
- Assignments can be followed through to completion
- Technical, task-oriented work, specialized area
- Noise and people at a minimum
- Close relationships with a small group of people
- Environment where quality and/or standards are important

POSSIBLE LIMITATIONS OF A HIGH C-OWL:

- Hesitate to act without precedent
- Overanalyze
- Be too critical of others
- Get bogged down in details
- Not verbalize feelings, but internalize them
- Be defensive when criticized
- Yield position to avoid controversy

POSSIBLE LIMITATIONS OF A HIGH C-OWL: *continued*
- Select people much like themselves
- Be too hard on themselves
- Tell ideas as opposed to sell ideas

Once you have identified the various behavior styles on your team, you know how to manage them better. The following are some tips for managing the various behavior styles:

MANAGING THE HIGH D:
- Clearly explain results expected
- Negotiate commitments one-on-one
- Define rules and show them where the limit is
- Confront face-to-face in all disagreements
- Provide challenging assignments
- Train on understanding and being easier on people
- Assist them in learning to pace self and relax
- Train on understanding teamwork and participation
- Train on listening skills
- Make sure their emotional intensity fits the situation

MANAGING THE HIGH I:
- Assist in setting realistic goals
- Work with on time management
- Develop a friendship and make time for interaction daily
- Have an open-door policy to discuss issues
- Train on behavioral styles to increase effective interactions
- Office them in a area where they can interact with others and get the job done
- Allow them freedom of movement, without any control
- Set clear objectives of task to be accomplished
- Look for opportunities for them to utilize their verbal skills

MANAGING THE HIGH S:

- Clearly explain changes
- Give rewards in terms of things
- Make an effort to get to know them and their needs
- Allow them to finish tasks they have started
- Assign them fewer, larger projects
- Encourage their contribution in meetings
- Involve them in the long-term planning
- Work to stretch them carefully to new heights
- Create a non-threatening environment, allowing disagreement
- Reward them for good work habits
- Clearly define parameters and requirements of a task
- Assign them to work with a small group of people
- Do not switch them from team to team
- Praise in public, rebuke gently in private

MANAGING THE HIGH C:

- Involve them in defining standards that are undefined
- Involve them in implementation of the standards
- Clearly define requirements of the job and expectations
- Allow them the opportunity to finish the tasks started
- Set goals that have "reach" in them
- Encourage their contribution in meetings
- Involve them in the long-term planning
- Train them in people skills and negotiating
- Respect their personal nature
- Office them in a less active area so they can work without interruptions
- Have them work with a small group of people
- Do not criticize their work unless you can prove a better way[2]

I also believe a great team is a group of people who don't just love the work they do, but also value and appreciate the people they have been called to work with. A true team functions as a family and lightens the load for everyone in the room because problems do not belong to "me" but rather they belong to "we!"

WHAT MAKES A GREAT TEAM?

- SAFE PLACE. There's a mutual exchange of support and needs being met within the team. It's a permission-based culture of honor where you can be yourself, share your needs, views and differences openly and others have permission to do the same. A safe environment that is free, open, and supportive of each other that can handle each other's mistakes.

- GOOD COMMUNICATION. The team openly communicates because of mutual trust and support as they share and listen to one another. Each one communicates clearly, adjusts and responds to what is needed in a timely manner.

- LOVING CONFRONTATIONS. The team accepts conflict and embraces the uncomfortable as necessary and desirable. They lovingly confront and work through conflicts openly as a team and tell the truth in a loving way that calls each other higher.

- CLEAR TEAM OBJECTIVES. No objective will be assumed by the team until clearly understood by all members. Everyone knows and takes responsibility for their part. As a team they stay focused on dreams of what could be rather than what was.[3]

- GIFTS DEFINED. Each individual's experience, abilities and gifts are fully utilized by the team. They accept wise counsel, support each other, recognize individual giftedness, and respect individual differences. This team is hungry to learn and open to new ways of thinking.[4]

CHAPTER 12

DISC in the Classroom

Honor is one of the most vital core values
for creating a safe place where people can be free
Honor protects the value that people have
for those who are different than they are.
~ Danny Silk ~

 had the privilege of going into my children's school to do some interactive DISC teambuilding classes with the seventh and eighth graders, high schoolers, and teachers. Target Training International, Ltd. offers a variety of DISCs, one of them being the Excellence for Learning DISC geared specifically for Teachers and Students. The teachers and students enjoyed learning about each other and gained a new language of understanding. It's fun to walk through the halls and still hear the kids referring to the DISC language as they interact with each other differently because of their experience.

With the students, I started out with the "Bird Exercise," which I explained previously. I had the teachers and students select which bird they identified with most before they received their assessments. Once they picked their birds, I had the students gather in their respective groups (Eagles, Parrots, Doves, Owls) at a table in each corner of the room for another exercise. I assigned the teachers to be observers. As observers I asked them to record everything that they saw, heard, and to make note of what the students did. Afterwards, the teachers shared with the class what they observed. I gave the students these instructions: "You have ten minutes to design a T-shirt logo and come up with a slogan that describes your group. Ready! Go!" It is absolutely hysterical to watch what plays out in the room. First of all, I only gave the D-Eagles a red and black marker because that's all they would need. In their group, the debates began immediately as to whose idea was the best. They were vigorously grabbing markers out of each other's hands. Finally, one of the students grabbed a marker, the paper, and just started drawing regardless of what the team was saying, because to the D-Eagles it's all about being the first to get done and win, even though that wasn't one of the instructions!

The I-Parrots never stopped talking and didn't even hear my instructions. Every single one of them grabbed a marker. In this group I provided a variety of colorful markers because I knew that's what they would like. All the while, they continued to laugh, talk, and immediately started coloring all over the paper randomly, with all the I-Parrots creatively expressing themselves. Three times they asked, "What are we supposed to be doing again?" They were definitely the hardest to keep focused and on task.

The S-Doves were standing back, accommodating one another, being friendly, no one really stepping up to take the lead. You could see each of them quietly processing, waiting for one of them to speak up and share an idea, yet wanting to let others go first. At one point, I walked over and assured them that it was alright if they didn't get anything on the paper before the time ran out.

By this time, the D-Eagles were already done with the I-Parrots coming in as a close second, and that side of the room was very loud as the D-Eagles were ready to move on to the next thing and the I-Parrots got even more energized and squirrelly.

The other side of the room was very quiet, mostly because they were just getting started because they had just finished their processing. I had to laugh—immediately after I gave the instructions the C-Owls were pulling me aside along with any teacher they could find to ask more questions to verify what exactly they were to accomplish. I purposely repeated the same instructions, kept things vague, and didn't answer any of their questions. I could see the confusion on their faces. I saw one of them go look for a pencil which I purposely did not provide, because I knew the C-Owls would want to sketch their idea on the back before they ever considered committing an idea to their T-shirt. Another went and got a dictionary to look up something. They barely finished in time.

When the timer went off, the S-Doves were still scrambling to get something on their T-shirt and kept going well after the timer went off. I had to ask them to put their markers down but before they could do so, they begged to finish what they were working on. You could see how overwhelmed they were by the exercise because they were so rushed.

These responses and dynamics typically play out in most workshop settings because the DISC characteristics and behaviors hold true to each behavior style. I have provided the samples of the T-shirts from the seventh and eighth grade class below. See if you can guess which one is the D-Eagle, I-Parrot, S-Dove and C-Owl:

T-shirts drawn by LifeAcademy 7th & 8th Graders.

Upper Left: S-Dove. Upper Right: D-Eagle. Lower Left: I-Parrot. Lower Right: C-Owl.

Then I taught them the DISC language and took them through their assessments. Once they had a grasp of the language, there were lots of fun activities that I did with them in each class. Another exercise was to have them get in their same groups again. This time the focus was on their opposite in the DISC. The assignment was for them to choose what type of car their opposite would drive and explain why. Then, as a group they had to create a bumper sticker with a saying that would best describe their opposite as well. As an example, the S-Doves would choose a car and create a bumper sticker that best describes the D-Eagle. The I-Parrots would choose one for the C-Owls and vice versa.

As homework between classes, I assigned them to observe their world—their family members, friends, teachers. Then in the next class, we really made it fun by getting into teams and playing games like "Name That Teacher." When it was their team's turn, the kids had to try to guess each teacher's DISC Behavior style in order to score points. If they gave the wrong answer, the other team could steal the point by providing the correct answer. We also played "Who Am I?" another game where I would read out the different DISC characteristics of a style and they had to guess which one it was.

One my favorite exercises to do with the kids is a "Puzzle Race." I have them get into four groups according to their strongest DISC characteristic around a table where there is twenty-five-piece puzzle. What they didn't know is that I mixed up all the pieces and even kept one piece from each so no one could win. The point of the exercise is that they all have to work together to complete their puzzle to win the race. Once again, I stationed the teachers throughout the room to observe, write down, and share what they saw throughout this exercise.

Immediately, we saw similar dynamics begin to play out. The D-Eagles were going as fast as they could, throwing pieces on the puzzle individually to win. Usually they are the first to realize the pieces are mixed up. Immediately they took off to the other groups to aggressively take back their pieces, while the Ds that remained at the table, hid the other team's pieces so they could't possibly win. The I-Parrots randomly ran around from table to table getting distracted by talking with everyone and created a party at every table they went to, never really getting much done. The S-Doves never moved the whole time. Everyone came to them and they spent most of their time happily finding the pieces that the others were needing in lieu of completing their own puzzle. It was so interesting to watch the C-Owls. None of them talked to each other; instead they were intently working on organizing all the pieces into groups by color, sorting out the corners, and putting the edges together first. They had their detailed system and eventually nominated one person to go find the other pieces. When it was all over and they realized that no one could win, I shared with them the point of this silly little exercise. The point wasn't only to figure out how to work together, but that each and every person is valuable. Each one of you are unique, valued, and have God-given talents and gifts. Each and every one of you is needed to make the puzzle complete. You bring to the table what others do not have. If a piece is missing, we all know it. At this time, I have a few of the students take turns reading aloud the passages of *One Body, Many Parts* from 1 Corinthians 12:12.

I love to conclude my workshops by taking time to celebrate each other. One of the exercises I did with the kids was to have them write down three strengths, talents, or gifts that they bring to this world on a paper puzzle piece cut out from a larger poster-size puzzle that they can hang in their classroom as a reminder. Once they have their name and the three things written down, I have them pair up and present each other's puzzle pieces to the class, so the class can thank and celebrate each student for who they are and what they bring to the kingdom of God.

The DISC exercises were so enlightening to the teachers. The light bulbs were going on. After one of the classes, a teacher came up to me so excited, "Now I understand my students so much better! This changes everything. This really helps me to know why certain students respond the way they do. I am more keenly aware of their styles and what they need so they can be more successful in my classroom. This will even change which students I seat where and how I form our groups from now on."

CONCLUSION

In conclusion, I hope what you have learned has helped you to understand your God-given design and that of others better so that you can honor and celebrate each other even more. That you have learned how to speak each other's language, know how to approach each other for a win-win encounter and to communicate more effectively. My hope has been that this book brought you into greater awareness of how God specifically created you and others so you can celebrate and step into all that God created you to be for His kingdom. That hopefully, this book has also fostered greater awareness of knowing how you are affecting those around you. I pray this has inspired you to create permission-based cultures of honor in which you and those you do life with have permission to freely express their needs and are willing to adjust to what is needed as well. As Danny Silk says in his book, *Culture of Honor*, "If you love me or care about me, it will show up in your response to what I told you was important to me. The way you manage yourself in our relationship is going to be a clear indicator. Adjusting your behavior to protect my heart is a true demonstration of love and honor."

Throughout *Understand Me, Understanding You* I have given you tools to improve your relationships, but they will only work if you apply them. As you begin to see results, you will be inspired to learn more—more about yourself and others. Getting to know and understand yourself and others is a lifetime pursuit, and it is worth the time.

Most of all I pray that the Spirit of revelation has opened your eyes to see yourself and others the way God originally intended. I pray that this is not the end but rather the beginning, and that revelation will continue throughout your life in every relationship. That you have an increased sense awareness and value for yourself, those you do life with, and especially for those who are not like you.

This is my continued prayer for you from Ephesians 1:17-23 (NIV):

I keep asking that the God of our Lord Jesus Christ, the glorious Father, may give you the Spirit of wisdom and revelation, so that you may know Him better. I pray that the eyes of your heart may be enlightened in order that you may know the hope to which He has called you, the riches of His glorious inheritance in His holy people, and His incomparably great power for us who believe.

In closing, you've learned! You've seen! You know! Now keep it at the forefront of your mind, practice it, step into it, walk in it, be intentional about it, develop it, and continue to transform all your relationships! I leave you with these questions:

- What will you do with what you have learned?
- How will you remember and apply what you have learned so you can see a difference in all your relationships and experience better connections?
- What will you do today? Tomorrow and the next day?

It's up to you to take it from here so that this information can produce transformation in your life!

God's blessings to you!
Wendy

ENDNOTES

Chapter 1: The Power of DISC Behaviors and Motivators

1. The Barna Group, Ltd. (2007) "Survey Reveals Challenges Faced by Young People" at *Barna Group*. www.barna.org/family-kids-articles/96-survey-reveals-challenges-faced-by-young-people

2. Target Training International, Ltd. (2011) "Chapter 1: What is DISC?" in *The Universal Language DISC Reference Manual*. (Scottsdale, AZ) 7-8.

3. Blueprint for Life, Inc. (2004) *Blueprint for Life™ – Discovering the Life you were Born to Live*. www.blueprintforlife.com.

Chapter 2: One Body, Many Parts

1. Peterson, Eugene H. (1993, 1994, 1995, 1996, 2000, 2001, 2002) *The Message* (Alive Communications, Inc.: Colorado Springs, CO)

2. Cooke, Graham (2012) Audio CD Disc 1: "How we are Known in Heaven" in *Living Your Truest Identity*. www.BrilliantBookHouse.com

3. Hetland, Leif (2011) *Seeing Through the Eyes of His Son* (Shippensburg, PA: Destiny Image Publishers) 67-68.

4. Kilpatrick, Bob and Joel (2010) *The Art of Being You* (WordServe Literary Group, Ltd., Highlands Ranch, CO)

Chapter 3: The Facet of Motivators

1. Bonnstetter, Bill and Bowers, Rick (1994-2004) "Chapter 1: History of Attitudes" in *TTI Personal Interests Attitudes and Values™ Certification Home Study Guide and Manual*. (Scottsdale, AZ) 3-4.

2. Ibid. P. 3.

Chapter 4: DISC Overview Flying at 60,000 Feet

1. Rosenberg, Merrick and Silvert, Daniel (2010) "Part II: The DISC Model" in *Taking Flight!* (Lexington, KY) 90-92.

2. Target Training International, Ltd. (2011) "Chapter 4: Defining & Learning the Language" in *The Universal Language DISC Reference Manual* (Scottsdale, AZ) 57-107.

Chapter 5: The Eight Sides of DISC Behaviors

1. Target Training International, Ltd. (2011) *The Universal Language DISC Reference Manual* (Scottsdale, AZ).

Chapter 6: Blending DISC Behavior Styles

1. Covey, Stephen (2004) *The 7 Habits of Highly Effective People* (New York, NY, Free Press).

Chapter 7: Speaking Each Other's Language

1. Covey, Stephen (2004) *The 7 Habits of Highly Effective People.* (New York, NY, Free Press).

2. Target Training International, Ltd. (2011) *The Universal Language DISC Reference Manual* (Scottsdale, AZ).

Chapter 8: Understanding the Insights® Graphs and Wheel

1. Collette, Tony (2013) "Know Yourself Quotes" at *Brainy Quote.* www.brainyquote.com/quotes/keywords/know_yourself

2. Target Training International, Ltd. (2011) *The Universal Language DISC Reference Manual* (Scottsdale, AZ).

3. Cooke, Graham (2012) Audio CD Disc 1: "How we are Known in Heaven." in *Living Your Truest Identity.* www.BrilliantBookHouse.com

4. Silk, Danny (2009) *Culture of Honor* (Shippensburg, PA: Destiny Image Publishers).

5. Silk, Danny (2008) *Loving our Kids on Purpose* (Shippensburg, PA: Destiny Image Publishers).

Chapter 9: Bringing DISC Home

1. Tutu, Desmond (2013) "Quotations about Family" at *Quote Garden.* www.quotegarden.com/family.html
2. Silk, Danny (2008) *Loving our Kids on Purpose* (Shippensburg, PA: Destiny Image Publishers).
3. DeSilva, Dawna and Liebshcer, Teresa (1998) *SOZO: Saved, Healed, Delivered–Basic.* www.bethelsozo.com to learn more about products and teachings.

Chapter 10: DISC Can Change Your Marriage

1. Meurer, Dave (2013) "Quotes on Marriage, Family, and Love" at *Marriage Moment.org.* www.marriagemoment.org/2011/10/quotes-on-marriage-family-and-love.html

2. Chapman, Gary (1995) *The Five Love Languages* (Chicago, IL: Northfield Publishing).

Chapter 11: DISC Can Transform Your Team

1. Silk, Danny (2009) *Culture of Honor* (Shippensburg, PA: Destiny Image Publishers).

2. Target Training International, Ltd. (2011) "Chapter 1: What is DISC?" in *The Universal Language DISC Reference Manual* (Scottsdale, AZ) 67.

3. Noble, Perry (2012) "What makes a great team?" at *Perry Noble* http://www.perrynoble.com/blog/what-makes-a-great-team

4. Covey, Stephen (2004) *The 7 Habits of Highly Effective People* (New York, NY, Free Press) 3.

Chapter 12: Using DISC in the Classroom

1. Silk, Danny (2009) *Culture of Honor* (Shippensburg, PA: Destiny Image Publishers).

2. Rosenberg, Merrick and Silvert, Daniel (2010) "Part II: The DISC Model" in *Taking Flight!* (Lexington, KY) 90-92.

Photo Credits

1. Google Images. *Crowded banquet hall at the Marriot.* www.lehmanlaw.com

2. Google Images. "Idea" *An open forum - Aberdare Town FC.* www.pitchero.com

3. Google Images. *Hare or Tortoise- Keep Yourself Focused and Motivated.* entrance-exam.net

4. Google Images. *Follow-the-rules* Get Busy Media. imagechef.com

RECOMMENDED READING & LISTENING

BOOKS:

Loving our Kids on Purpose – Danny Silk

Culture of Honor – Danny Silk

The 7 Habits of Highly Effective People – Stephen Covey

Seeing Through Heaven's Eyes – Leif Hetland

*The Five Love Language*s – Gary Chapman

Dream Culture – Andy and Janine Mason

Powerful and Free – Danny Silk

Taking Flight! – Merrick Rosenberg and Daniel Silvert

When Heaven Invades Earth – Bill Johnson

Strengthen Yourself in the Lord – Bill Johnson

The Essential DISC Training Workbook – Jason Hedge

The Universal Language DISC Reference Manual – Bill Bonnstetter and Judy Suiter

AUDIO TEACHING:

Living Your Truest Identity – Graham Cooke

Keys to Confrontation – Danny Silk

People Helping People – Danny Silk

Insert Love Here – Sheri Silk

The Art of Thinking Brilliantly – Graham Cooke

Defining The Relationship – Danny Silk